ADVANCE PRAISE FOR

I enthusiastically recommend *Lead Your Way* to anyone who is interested in practical, balanced advice about what you can do right now to progress in your career. This book will help you increase your self-awareness and be thoughtful and strategic about your career. It contains rich illustrative examples and useful exercises to help you move into action.

> Chris Simmons, U.S. Leadership Team Member, Managing Partner –
> Washington Metro Region, and Chief Diversity Officer, PwC (retired)

If you want to create a truly fulfilling career, then *Lead Your Way* is the book for you. Karen Watai shows you how to set yourself up for success by understanding what you are about, doing the necessary preparation, and maximizing your career opportunities. The strategies, exercises, and illustrative insights she provides bring these concepts to life.

> —Carol Fulp, President and CEO, The Partnership, Inc.

For those who can't work with Karen Watai directly, this book is the next best thing. The exercises and examples highlight the importance of creating an authentic career based on your personal values, and provide guidance on developing the rich relationships necessary for a rewarding career.

> —Michael Molinaro, Vice President and Chief Learning Officer, New York Life

Karen Watai has written a book which acknowledges the realities of the workplace and is designed to help everyone be more successful in their careers. *Lead Your Way* recognizes that the workplace is not a level playing field, and helps individuals create more satisfying careers by acting in alignment with their values, strengths, and interests.

> —Freada Kapor Klein, Founder and Board Chair, Level Playing Field Institute;
> Co-Chair, Kapor Center for Social Impact; Partner, Kapor Capital

LEAD YOUR WAY

Practical
Coaching Advice
for Creating the
Career You Want

KAREN J. WATAI

 Business Mastery Press

Printed and bound in the United States of America
ISBN: 978-0-692-97521-3
Library of Congress Control Number: 2017917396

To my Dad and Mom, who
gave me the best foundation of all.

To my children Scott, Alex, and Elizabeth, who
bring love, joy, and wisdom to my life.

To my clients, who
have so generously shared their journeys with me
and who are the inspiration for this book.

TABLE OF CONTENTS

Part III. Opportunity

FOREWORD

*Y*ou *are the only person who can effectively manage and drive your career.* In today's world of constant change and challenge, where markets and organizations shift overnight, where people move quickly between jobs and organizations, either you are managing and driving your career or you have ceded control of your career to others.

When I began my career in 1986, I was initially interested in three topics: how people manage their careers, the influence of race on opportunities, and how organizations change. As a professor at the Harvard Business School and the Wharton School at the University of Pennsylvania, I spent years researching these topics and publishing my findings. I worked with thousands of business school students, as well as managers and executives. In my administrative roles as President of Morehouse College and Dean of Georgetown University's McDonough School of Business, I rolled up my sleeves and moved into the role of a practitioner.

I have researched careers, counseled others on their careers, and managed my own. I have identified the key factors that contribute to career success, as well as the challenges which must be overcome. And I know the value of having the support and guidance of an experienced mentor and coach.

That's where this book comes in. Karen has written the practical how-to manual, based on my research, for anyone who wants to maximize their career. As you read this book, you will be hearing her voice speaking to you. Karen will be your coach. She will point you in the right direction, share critical information, ask you the right questions, and help you make the best decisions.

She will share her insights and advice, as well as the strategies, tactics, and approaches she has honed over years of working with clients just like you. As your coach, Karen's only objective is to help you reach your career goals.

I've known Karen for more than 25 years. We first worked together when she was at Goldman Sachs. When she left her career in finance and became an executive coach, we reconnected and began a collaboration that lasts to this day. I have been struck by her insightful and practical approach to helping her clients achieve their goals. She is well versed in the realities of the workplace, and brings her business experience into her coaching. Her ability to engage and bring out the best in her clients is extraordinary.

If you are about to graduate from college or graduate school, this book is for you. If you are just starting out in a new job, this book is for you. If you are aspiring to become a manager or move into the executive ranks, this book is for you. If you are considering a change or transition, this book is for you. And if you are a new executive, this book will remind you of what you need to do for continued success.

You are the only one who can effectively manage and drive your career. Read on. Learn. Move into action. Create the career you want.

David A. Thomas, President of Morehouse College, H. Naylor Fitzhugh Professor Emeritus of Business Administration at the Harvard Business School, former Dean of Georgetown University's McDonough School of Business

INTRODUCTION

Y*ou leap out of bed on Monday morning, excited to start your day. You enjoy thinking about work, even on your days off. Your work is something you* **want** *to do, instead of something you* **have** *to do.*

This doesn't have to be a dream.

If this is how you want to feel about your career, if you are open to guidance and willing to put in the effort, then this book is for you. You'll find a research-based framework for moving your career forward. There are exercises and assessments to help you apply the framework and there are suggestions, strategies, and techniques to help you achieve your career goals.

You are a unique individual with your own experiences, perspectives, and desires, and I am here to guide you and help you make your own best decisions. As you read this book, imagine that I am your personal executive coach and I am talking directly to you. My only agenda is to provide information, ask questions, listen without judgment, and help you accomplish your goals. I am sharing with you the same information I use with great success in my career development workshops and with my individual coaching clients.

You will hear many stories throughout this book. All of these are based on the experiences of real people and are designed to illustrate some of the most common themes I've encountered in my work. Some are composites, and all are disguised. These are the stories of people like you—people who were motivated to take their careers further.

The Framework

The framework for this book is based on research and derived from my experience working with thousands of clients over the years. It applies to everyone, and contains additional information for members of underrepresented groups, including women, people of color, and others who are different in some way from the leadership of their organization.

There are several principles embedded in this framework. They are:

1. **Luck happens when preparation meets opportunity.** This book is about how to be luckier in your career by being better prepared to recognize, create, and maximize your opportunities. If you're reading this book, it is likely that you are just starting out, not moving as fast as you'd like, or not heading in the direction you want to go. Taking the proactive steps discussed in this book will help you be luckier in your career.

2. **Always be authentic and true to yourself.** Nothing else works in the long term. Living your life in alignment with what's truly important to you brings fulfillment, energy, and purpose. Other people can see this alignment and will find you much more compelling in what you do. When people try to be someone or something they are not, it is difficult to keep up the charade and, more often than not, other people can see right through it. Always lead your way.

3. **It is important to know where you want to go, so you can head in the right direction.** One of the most significant questions for you to answer is "What do you want?" You need to be driving toward your goals, and it's essential that your goals are in alignment with your values, strengths, and interests. When you are clear on your goals, you will be better equipped to make decisions at critical junctures in your career. When your goals are in alignment with who you are, you will have more

energy and determination to reach them. Doing the exercises in this book will help you formulate goals that are meaningful for you.

4. **Focus on what you *can* control.** Sometimes life happens to us. There are things in each of our lives over which we have no control. Your power rests in your willingness and ability to focus on what you *can* control.

5. **There are no guarantees.** You can do everything suggested in this book, and still be stymied by the organizational culture you work in, a problematic manager, sudden changes in the industry or market, or yet another corporate reorganization. These are factors outside of your control. If you're in such a situation, then following the framework outlined in this book and paying attention to what *is* under your control is all the more critical in order to be as lucky as possible in your career.

6. **You are a whole person.** Think about what you want in your career in the context of your whole life. Think about the sacrifices you are willing or not willing to make. Think about your priorities at each stage of your life, and make conscious decisions to create the whole life you desire.

How This Book Is Organized

This book is organized in three parts:

Part I—Foundation begins with a chapter illustrating how all the concepts in this book work together. It then guides you through a series of exercises to help you identify your values, strengths, interests, and goals.

Part II—Preparation takes you through what you need to focus on to move forward—namely competence, credibility, relationships, and confidence. In addition, it offers information on challenges faced by people who are different from those at the top of their organizations, and looks at limiting beliefs that can hold people back from performing at their highest level.

Part III—Opportunity addresses how to recognize and create career opportunities, as well as how to determine whether, when, and how to move on. In the final chapter, you will put it all together and create your own Career Game Plan.

How to Use This Book

This book is meant to be lived. Reading is just the start. Real learning and progress will happen when you move into action. At the end of each chapter, you will find a Summary of Key Points and a Personal Takeaways section. Use the Personal Takeaways section to record your insights as well as the specific actions you will take to move your career forward.

Once you take action, reflect on your experience. Ask yourself what worked and what didn't, what you want to repeat and what you won't do again. Learn from your experiences, and apply that learning going forward.

You can either read this book front to back, or you can read the chapters that address your specific issues and concerns. Recognize that your career journey will have twists and turns. Come back to this book periodically. Review these concepts as new situations arise. Reassess your goals. Touch base with your values, strengths, and interests. Update your Career Game Plan. Keep learning. Stay prepared. Keep your eyes open for opportunities. Lead your way and create the career you want.

OPPORTUNITY

PREPARATION

FOUNDATION

Part I:
FOUNDATION

Chapter 1

SETTING THE STAGE

Lee has had a long and successful career.

"I've been really lucky," says Lee. "I love the work I do. I wanted to run a business, and I got the chance to do it. I was pretty good at the work and people believed in me. They trusted me and gave me the chance to do more. I know a lot of people at my company and I've really liked most of them. They knew I wanted to run one of our business units and, as it turns out, I got to head up one of our divisions for many years. I couldn't have asked for more."

Many people attribute their own success to luck—to being in the right place at the right time. But what is luck, and what can people do to increase their chances of being lucky? Let's take a closer look at Lee's story and examine more deeply what actually happened in Lee's career.

"I've been really lucky."

Lee attributes a successful career to luck. In reality, Lee's luck was the result of preparation meeting opportunity. Lee was prepared and therefore able to recognize, create, and maximize opportunities.

"I love the work I do."

Lee's work aligned with Lee's values, strengths, and interests. When you have this level of congruence between who you are and the work you do, work becomes a pleasure. You are more likely to find your work fulfilling, to have the energy to learn and perform at a high level, and to persevere when faced with challenging situations. Chapter 2 includes exercises to help you identify your values, strengths, and interests.

"I wanted to run a business, and I got the chance to do it."

Lee had clear goals. Lee wanted to run a business. When you have goals, you are better able to share your goals with others, proactively develop the skills that will help you succeed, and choose a path that will lead you in the direction you want to go. Chapter 3 will help you set your own career goals.

"I was pretty good at the work and people believed in me. They trusted me and gave me the chance to do more."

Lee developed and demonstrated a high degree of competence and mastery. Lee earned a reputation for high performance and integrity, which led others to believe in Lee and trust Lee with critical growth assignments and additional responsibilities. Chapters 4 and 5 will help you assess and create a plan to develop your competence and credibility.

"I know a lot of people at my company and I've really liked most of them."

Lee put a premium on getting to know people in the company on both a professional and personal level. Lee took an interest in learning about them and what they did, and built deep and diverse relationships across the organization. The people Lee connected with shared information, gave advice, and helped create opportunities for Lee to learn and grow. As Lee's competence, credibility, and relationships grew, Lee's confidence also grew.

Chapters 6 and 7 address building relationships and the importance of confidence in progressing in your career.

"They knew I wanted to run one of our business units and, as it turns out, I got to head up one of our divisions for many years."

Lee let the decision makers and influencers in the company know that Lee's goal was to run a business unit. When offered opportunities to work in different parts of the business, Lee accepted the positions that would help build knowledge and skills essential to running a business. Lee also volunteered to work on strategic projects related to the business. Lee both recognized the opportunities that were presented *and* created more. Chapter 10 addresses recognizing and creating opportunities.

What Lee did *not* say.

Based on the above, you might think Lee's career developed smoothly. But, Lee did not mention the challenges and obstacles along the way.

There is no mention of the number of times Lee changed jobs or considered changing jobs—whether because of a call from a headhunter, a desire for something different, or feeling stymied at work. Chapter 11 addresses making the decision of whether, when, and how to move on.

Lee did not talk about prejudice and bias in the workplace; or how it sometimes was difficult to connect with people; or that it took longer to get to the same place than some colleagues. These are challenges faced by many people who differ in some way from those at the top of an organization. Chapter 8 discusses these organizational challenges and how to address them.

We did not hear about the self-doubt and limiting beliefs that might have stalled Lee's career. Many people have limiting beliefs that, unless addressed, can hold them back from performing at their highest level. Chapter 9 focuses on these challenges from within and offers strategies to overcome them.

Lee's story illustrates the many actions you can take to be luckier in your career. In today's world of constant change, it is more important than ever to take control of your career. Chapter 12 guides you through a template to create a Career Game Plan.

You may have noticed that you cannot discern Lee's gender, ethnicity, background, or any other aspect of identity from this story. That is because Lee could be anyone. Lee could be you.

Chapter 2

VALUES, STRENGTHS, AND INTERESTS

What motivates you? What are you good at? What grabs and holds your attention? These are your values, strengths, and interests, and when your work aligns with all three, you've hit the career trifecta. You are more likely to find your work fulfilling, to have the energy to learn and perform at a high level, and to persevere when faced with challenging situations.

Understanding your values, strengths, and interests provides a powerful foundation for making career decisions. If you are just starting out in your career, look for work and an organization that align with your values, strengths, and interests. If you are considering a move to a new team or organization, think about the new group's culture, and whether the new opportunity leverages your values, strengths, and interests.

Meet Mike and Ana. Their stories illustrate the difference between being in a job that fits your values, strengths, and interests, and one that does not.

> **Mike:** Mike worked as a software developer at a large technology company. He was working on a project to decrease the processing time for a particular application. While he knew it was important, he didn't like the fact that he was only fine-tuning an existing process and not creating something new. While talented technically, Mike had always thought that his real strengths were in coming up with new ideas for products. He really enjoyed reading and thinking about the needs of

the customer and wished he could do something that was more about creating innovative new customer experiences. Mike wasn't happy in his job, and was thinking about making a move.

Ana: After high school, Ana got a job as a receptionist at a manufacturing company. She was bored, and curious about other jobs at the company. Ana loved a challenge, and when she overheard a friend in the controller's office talk about how no one could figure something out, she asked if she could try it. She had always been good with numbers. To her amazement, her friend said yes and explained what they were trying to do. Ana worked all weekend, figured it out, and brought the completed work back to her friend. She was soon recruited into a position in the controller's office. Ana earned her college degree and eventually worked her way up to becoming a controller. She found the industry fascinating and never grew tired of the challenge of accounting. Ana loved her job and thrived in her career.

Mike was unhappy in his job; Ana loved her job. Mike's values included creativity, his strengths lay in coming up with new ideas for products, and he was interested in the customer experience. His work was not in alignment with his values, strengths, and interests. Ana's work, on the other hand, was in alignment with her value of being challenged, her strength with numbers, and her interest in the industry and the business. She had hit the career trifecta.

This chapter is designed to help you set a foundation for going forward, and is composed of exercises for you to complete. If you already know and can articulate your values, strengths, and interests, record them in the Personal Takeaways section at the end of this chapter. If not, use these exercises to gain a deeper understanding of your values, strengths, and interests.

Personal Values Identification

Personal values will help you lead your way. Your personal values are those things that are so important to you that they literally compel or motivate your behavior. They are the invisible *why* behind what you do. When you can shine a light on your motivators and understand them, you can use them as touchstones for making decisions. The decisions you make that are in alignment with your values are the ones that will feel right, and the ones that will lead to more energy and engagement as you move into action. Here are two examples of how personal values were used to make career decisions:

Kevin: Through exercises and reflection, Kevin learned that above all he valued social justice, recognition, and making an impact. Kevin received multiple job offers after law school. After consulting his values, Kevin decided to join a law firm with a social justice practice. He also liked the fact that this law firm had a star culture which recognized individual contributions. He knew he would prefer this culture to one which treated everyone the same.

Jasmine: Jasmine identified her top three values as achievement, creativity, and helping people. She realized that her job in HR aligned perfectly with all three values. When Jasmine was offered a job in compliance, with a higher salary, she turned it down. She knew that the increased compensation wasn't worth as much to her as being able to do work that was so closely aligned with her values.

Some of the most difficult career decisions arise when there is a conflict between what you want in your professional life and what you want in your personal life. Greg, in the example below, had to wrestle with this conflict.

Greg: Greg's top values were faith, family, and achievement. When he was offered a promotion to a widely-coveted position that would require significant travel, Greg decided to turn down the opportunity because it would interfere with his church and family responsibilities. Greg continues to be a high performer at his company while remaining at the same level. Greg knew that turning down the promotion might limit his career prospects, but he decided that his church activities and time with his family were more important than moving up.

The following exercise is designed to help you identify and articulate your values by analyzing experiences that you found especially fulfilling. Here are two examples of how this exercise helped people identify their values:

Mary: Mary identified her college years as a particularly meaningful and satisfying time in her life. She described it like this: "I loved college, and not for the reason you might think. It had nothing to do with my classes. I did so many things for the first time. I joined the soccer team and had a blast learning and playing soccer with great teammates. I went skiing for the first time with my roommates. I made lifelong friends." As Mary examined these experiences, she uncovered two of her values— adventure or doing new things, and connecting with people.

Anthony: Anthony identified an experience playing tennis as one of his most meaningful. He described it like this: "I remember one of my tennis matches. There was a lot at stake and I was playing the number one seed in the tournament. I won the first set, and then I felt my back tightening up. There was no way I was going to give up, so I battled through it. I had to win the second set because I didn't think I could make it through a third set. I put all my energy into making every stroke count, and ended up winning. Even though I was in incredible pain, I felt great." Anthony easily identified three of his personal values in this experience—competition, challenge, and achievement.

The following exercise is in three parts. In Part 1, you will identify three of your own meaningful experiences in different contexts. In Part 2, you will analyze the common themes, and in Part 3, you will use these themes to identify your personal values.

EXERCISE: PERSONAL VALUES IDENTIFICATION

PART I. Meaningful Experiences

Experience I. Describe a moment or an experience that felt particularly meaning-ful and satisfying, and that left you feeling positive and energized. Think about an experience in the context of *work or school*.

Where were you?

What were you doing?

Who were you with?

What was your purpose or objective?

What was it about this experience that made it so fulfilling?

Experience 2. Describe a moment or an experience that felt particularly meaningful and satisfying, and that left you feeling positive and energized. Think about an experience in the context of *community involvement or a hobby*.

Where were you?

What were you doing?

Who were you with?

What was your purpose or objective?

What was it about this experience that made it so fulfilling?

Experience 3. Describe a moment or an experience that felt particularly meaningful and satisfying, and that left you feeling positive and energized. Think about an experience in the context of *your personal life, family life, or relationships.*

Where were you?

What were you doing?

Who were you with?

What was your purpose or objective?

What was it about this experience that made it so fulfilling?

PART 2. Analyzing Themes

What made these three experiences so fulfilling for you?

Look for the themes in your description of what made these experiences so fulfilling. These themes encapsulate your personal values. Use a word or a phrase to describe each theme below.

PART 3. Personal Values

Now, come up with a list of your personal values stated in the most concise way possible. Limit yourself to no more than five personal values.

Now that you've identified your values, pay attention to how they play out in your daily life. Notice how your values influence your behaviors and decisions. Use your values as touchstones when you have an important decision to make. Values tend to be consistent over time, but can change as a result of life experiences and circumstances, so come back to this exercise periodically and reassess your values.

Strengths

Everyone has strengths. These are the authentic talents, abilities, and skills that often lead to high levels of performance in a particular area. Doing work that capitalizes on your strengths will increase the likelihood that you will thrive in your career. If your strengths lie in understanding numbers and data, an analyst position may suit you well. If your strengths lie in working with people, a sales or management position may suit you well.

The following exercise will help you identify your natural talents, abilities, and skills by looking back at actual experiences you have had. Let's go back to Mary and Anthony from the previous section, and hear how they describe their strengths.

Mary: "If you had asked me what my strengths were in college, I would have said that they were having fun and making friends. After I started working, I realized that I had a knack for building high-performing, collaborative teams. I find new challenges exciting, build great relationships, and can inspire a team to work together to accomplish some really difficult tasks."

Anthony: "I'm really good under pressure. I stay calm, see clearly, and execute. In my job in IT, I'm the go-to guy when a customer system goes down. Every second our system is down costs us money and customer satisfaction, so the stakes are high. In a crisis, I'm the one that everyone relies on to quickly analyze the situation and figure out a solution."

EXERCISE: STRENGTHS IDENTIFICATION

PART I. Answer the following questions.

Review the three experiences you listed in the Personal Values Identification exercise. What are the talents, abilities, and skills you used in each of these situations?

Think about other situations in which you were able to do things better, faster, or more easily than most other people. What talents, abilities, and skills did you use to reach the high levels of performance you attained?

What are the talents, abilities, and skills that other people frequently and consistently compliment you on?

What do people frequently and consistently ask you to help them with?

PART 2. Examine the talents, abilities, and skills that you described in part 1. List your top five strengths below. Be as specific as you can in your description.

1.

2.

3.

4.

5.

You may not be aware of all your strengths. When you can do something well without any conscious effort, you may not realize that it is in fact one of your strengths. You may also not be aware that you have a particular strength if you haven't yet had an experience that required you to use that strength. Once you work through this exercise, ask a few people who know you well for their thoughts on your strengths. They may help you identify some strengths of which you haven't been aware.

Interests

Imagine you're an accountant who loves fast cars. Would you rather have a career as a controller at a pet food company, or would you rather be a controller at Ferrari?

Bringing your interests into your career increases your level of engagement. An interest is a subject or activity that draws your attention and captivates you. You find yourself naturally wanting to learn more about and be involved in your area of interest. Working in an area that relates to one of your interests will inevitably engage you more than working in an area that does not.

The following exercise will help you identify your interests by looking back at subjects or activities that you have found compelling and engaging. Let's hear how Mary and Anthony identified their interests through this exercise.

Mary: "I'm still really active—I ski with my friends and I'm on the company softball team. My favorite magazines are either health-related or, frankly, *Harvard Business Review*. I love learning about leadership and culture, and those are the articles that grab my attention. My favorite subject in business school was organizational behavior. I guess you can say my interests include sports, people, and leadership."

Anthony: "I sort of have two sides to myself. On the one hand, I'm still an athlete. On the other hand, I'm really a nerd. My favorite subject in school was data analytics. I read everything I can find on data analytics, and I love staying up to date on everything that's happening in my industry. My overriding interest is really technology."

EXERCISE: INTERESTS IDENTIFICATION

PART I. Answer the following questions.

What do you enjoy doing in your free time?

What kinds of books, magazines, and websites do you like to read? What holds your interest from beginning to end?

What do you like to learn about?

What were your favorite subjects in school?

What aspect of your current or past jobs have you found particularly compelling and engaging?

PART 2. What themes emerged in your answers to the above questions? Use these themes to identify your interests and list them here. Add any others that come to mind.

Summary of Key Points

- When your work is in alignment with your personal values, strengths, and interests, you are more likely to find your work fulfilling, to have the energy to learn and perform at a high level, and to persevere when faced with challenging situations.
- Personal values reflect those things that are so important to you that they literally compel or motivate your behavior. When you act in alignment with your values, you experience a high degree of energy, engagement, and fulfillment.
- Strengths are areas in which you have the ability to consistently achieve high levels of performance. Doing work that capitalizes on your strengths increases the likelihood that you will thrive.
- Interests are subjects or activities that draw your attention and captivate you. Working in an area of interest increases your level of engagement.
- Use your values, strengths, and interests as touchstones for making career decisions.

Personal Takeaways

Record your insights and respond to the question on the following page.

PERSONAL VALUES	STRENGTHS	INTERESTS

Think of a current or upcoming career decision. How can you use your personal values, strengths, and interests as touchstones for this decision?

Chapter 3

GOALS

What do you want? This is one of the most important questions for you to answer. Once you know what you want, you can move intentionally in that direction.

Ben, Teresa, and Christine approached this question in three different ways.

Ben: After Business School, Ben began his career at a large consulting firm. He knew he wanted to make partner and, within a few years, decided that his real goal was to run the firm. Ben made decisions from day one that he believed would lead him to partnership and to an executive position—he transferred into areas where he saw greater opportunity, he built relationships and talked about his aspirations with senior people, and he seized every opportunity that he believed would help him reach his goal of heading up the firm.

Teresa: In college, Teresa's favorite classes were in finance and game theory. She interned at an investment bank and, while she thought the work was interesting, she did not appreciate the brutal hours. After graduating, she joined a private equity firm where, as she put it, "I can do interesting work and I don't have to work every weekend." She spent four years at the private equity firm and decided that, in addition to interesting work and more civilized hours, she also wanted to work in an environment that was more supportive, with a manager who cared about her development, and where she could really grow professionally. She spent six months searching for the right position, and ended up working at a hedge fund that met all her requirements.

Christine: Christine's goal in life had been to go to a top college and graduate school, and she did. When it came time to make a career decision, she ended up joining a prestigious tech company because, at the time, that was the most coveted position among her classmates. She meandered through her time at the company, moving about reactively rather than proactively. While Christine had been goal-directed in her education, she had never thought to set goals for her career.

What happened to these three people? Ben did end up running the firm. Teresa continued to craft her life around her priorities. And Christine, after years of meandering in her career, finally learned the value of knowing what she wanted and going after it.

Ben knew exactly where he wanted to end up. Teresa knew what was important to her and used that as a list of nonnegotiables as she looked for jobs. And Christine drifted in her career until she decided what she really wanted.

In my work with clients, I have seen two kinds of goals—destination and directional goals. Ben had a destination goal, while Teresa had a directional goal. Each resonates with different people. Destination goals are specific, time-bound goals set by people who know exactly what they want at a specific point in the future. In contrast, directional goals are set by people who may not know exactly what they want in the future, but know what they *need* to be happy and fulfilled. These directional goals take the form of nonnegotiable requirements for their career. A destination goal might sound like, "I want to be a partner in tax at a major accounting firm." A directional goal might sound like, "I don't know exactly where I want to end up, but I want to be interacting with people and I want to be working in the tax field."

I have also found that people generally gravitate toward one of two time frames when they set their goals. Some people most easily focus on long-term goals, while others focus more easily on short-term goals. When asked about what they want, some people's immediate response is to think several steps or years ahead, while others focus on the next step or level. Either one of these approaches can work for you.

If you are someone who focuses on the long term, create short-term goals that will be the steppingstones that lead you to your long-term objective. If you are someone who focuses on the short term, I encourage you to act in a way that keeps your future options open so that you can ultimately go for any goal you decide upon in the future.

The following exercise is in three parts. Part 1 is designed to spark ideas and gather insights into what you want. Part 2 will help you create specific short-term and long-term goals, and Part 3 will help you refine your goals. If you are already clear on your goals, record them in the Personal Takeaways section at the end of this chapter.

EXERCISE: SETTING CAREER GOALS

PART I. Gathering Insights

Imagine that it is 10 or 20 years from now and you have fulfilled all your career dreams. What would you have done?

Imagine that it is one year from now and you are thrilled and celebrating an extraordinarily successful year. What would you have done?

When you were a child, what did you want to be when you grew up? What was it about that job that you found appealing? Do you still find it appealing today?

Think about the people you know. What do they do? Do they enjoy their jobs? If you could, would you trade places with any of them? What is it about that other position that appeals to you?

PART 2. Establishing Goals

Review your responses to the questions in Part 1. Notice the themes that emerge from your responses to these questions. Now, answer the following questions:

What do you want long-term? Be as specific as you can.

What do you want short-term? Be as specific as you can.

PART 3. Refining Your Goal

Review the long-term and short-term goals you developed in Part 2 and consider the following:

- Do your short-term goals lead you in the direction of your long-term goals?

- Do your goals align with your values, strengths, and interests?

If not, refine your goals to bring them into alignment, and record them here.

Summary of Key Points

- Once you know what you want, you can proactively and intentionally take steps to move in that direction.
- Destination goals are specific, time-bound goals set by people who know exactly what they want at a specific point in the future.
- Directional goals are set by people who may not know exactly what they want in the future, but know what they *need* to be happy and fulfilled. These directional goals take the form of nonnegotiable requirements for their career.
- If you are someone who focuses on the long term, create short-term goals that will be the steppingstones that lead you to your long-term objectives. If you are someone who focuses on the short term, act in a way that keeps your options open to ultimately go for any goal you decide upon in the future.
- Parts II and III of this book will help you think through the steps you can take to accomplish your goals.

Personal Takeaways

Record your insights on the following page.

Long-Term Goals:

Short-Term Goals:

OPPORTUNITY

PREPARATION

FOUNDATION

Part II:
PREPARATION

Chapter 4

COMPETENCE

A consistently high level of competence and performance makes a world of difference when it comes to long-term career success. Developing a deep level of expertise, continually mastering new skills, and learning from your experiences and feedback are essential.

I have met many people who believe that if they work hard and do good work, they will be rewarded. Too many of these people are disappointed when they do not receive a promotion, recognition, or increased compensation. Doing good work is not enough. In addition, it's important to master communication, influence, leadership, and political skills, and follow the guidance outlined in this book.

Communication skills involve connecting with people, listening to understand, and conveying your messages effectively. Influence skills involve being able to convince or inspire people to act. Leadership skills result in people wanting to follow you and work toward your vision. Political skills are about being able to get things done when you need people with varying interests to contribute toward achieving a desired objective. When I talk to people who have a negative reaction to "political skills," it is generally because they are assuming it means working toward an unethical end goal, and/or reaching an end goal in an unethical way. I encourage you to think about political skills as being the skills you need to ethically influence a group of people with disparate interests to work together toward an ethical end goal.

There are many ways to learn and develop your skills. You can learn from developmental experiences. You can learn from classes, training sessions, and reading. You can learn from informal conversations with others, and you can learn from candid, constructive feedback.

Learning from Developmental Experiences

You can build competence through high-quality developmental experiences that take you outside of your comfort zone and challenge you to build additional skills. These experiences might include taking on additional responsibilities, accepting a stretch assignment, or participating in a task force or special project.

Here are three examples of learning from developmental experiences.

Phebe: Phebe was an individual contributor who wanted to move into management. She asked to manage her department's two summer interns. She talked to others who had managed summer interns before to get their advice, and she was deliberate and thoughtful about how she onboarded the interns, gave them assignments, coached them, and evaluated them. At the end of the summer, she reflected on her experience and made a list of things she would do when she became a manager, and a list of things she would not.

Susan: Susan was a Vice President in a technology company. She had spent her career in one area of the organization, and wanted to expand her knowledge base to better understand other areas. When she heard that a task force was being formed to address a strategic challenge faced by the company, she volunteered. Through her work with the task force, she developed a deeper understanding of the market, the competitive landscape, and the business. She also developed new relationships with people throughout the organization.

Gabriel: Gabriel was in his third year at an accounting firm. Knowing he wanted to make partner, Gabriel was intent on learning business development skills as soon as possible. He volunteered to help one of the partners on a new business opportunity, and attended the client pitch meeting so he could observe and learn. He was soon volunteering for other new business opportunities and asking to be a part of the presentation.

Be on the lookout for developmental experiences and assignments that allow you to develop your technical and social skills, competencies, and knowledge base.

Learning from Classes, Reading, and Informal Conversations with Others

You can learn by attending formal programs offered by universities, your employer, or other organizations. There are programs presented in person, and others that are offered virtually. There are countless opportunities to learn from books and the internet. You can also learn informally from other people. Regardless of how you learn, it is critical to leverage what you learn to benefit and add value to your work and your organization.

Meet Laura and Andres. Notice how they used what they learned to enhance their competence and add value to their organizations.

Laura: Laura had been a Director in Human Resources before moving to a Diversity position in her company. To be more effective in her new position, Laura wanted more of an understanding of the diversity field and asked her company for more training.

Her company agreed, and paid for her to attend a Diversity and Inclusion Professionals Certificate program. Laura was able to leverage her training by creating more informed strategic plans, bringing diversity best practices to her organization, and implementing innovative programs.

Andres: Andres was a young associate in corporate finance at an investment bank. He was so interested in learning about companies and their businesses that, in his free time, he studied offering prospectuses. He brought his deep understanding of industries and companies to his work in corporate finance, and stood out as someone with extraordinary expertise in analyzing businesses. His firm ultimately asked him to transfer to a new high-growth area where he could use this knowledge more directly.

Learning through informal conversations with other people provides several ancillary benefits. When talking to others within your organization, you may end up learning not only about the topic you raised, but also about the history, politics, and peculiarities of your organization. When talking to people outside of your organization, you may learn more about your competition, the industry, and market trends. In both cases, you may also establish deeper relationships with people that could be helpful as you move through your career.

Here are three examples of learning from informal conversations:

Brianna: Brianna was just starting out in her career and wanted to master the technical aspects of her job. She was working in the same field as her college major and soon found that what she had learned in college wasn't enough. She had so many questions. She made it a practice to find someone who was an expert at whatever she was interested in learning, and ask them for help.

Alex: Alex was a Vice President who had just taken on responsibility for a much broader scope of the business. He received feedback that he needed to develop better influence skills across the organization. Realizing that he needed help, he sought out an experienced Senior Vice President as a mentor to guide and counsel him. Alex was able to learn from his mentor's political savvy and deep understanding of the organization and key stakeholders.

Steven: Steven was the Chief Operating Officer of an organization in the midst of high growth and change. He wanted to be the most effective leader he could be. He enlisted the help of an executive coach to help him deepen his self-awareness, think through the needs of the organization, and develop strategies and skills to lead the organization through a challenging period.

Learning from Feedback

Timely, specific, and candid feedback is essential for your development. It helps you understand what you're doing well and what you need to work on. It helps you assess whether your actions are having the impact you intend, and whether you are making the career progress you desire. If you're getting accurate and candid real-time feedback, there should be no surprises at review, compensation, or promotion time.

If you're not receiving feedback, ask for it. You can ask for general feedback, or for feedback around a specific interaction or situation. You can ask for feedback from your manager, another senior person, a peer, or someone else with whom you have interacted. Identify the appropriate person, and find a time and place where you can have a conversation without distractions. Let them know that you are working on your career development, and value their opinion. Ask them what you did well and what you can do to improve. Listen to learn—manage any impulse you may have to argue, defend, explain, or tell the other person they are wrong. Ask clarifying questions, such as "Can you give me an example of that?" or "Can you help me understand that better?" Then thank them for sharing this information with you. After you receive feedback, synthesize the information, learn from it, and decide how best to act on it. If possible, follow up and let the other person know how helpful their feedback was.

Meet Sophia. Her story illustrates how accurate feedback can help to identify critical development areas.

Sophia: Sophia wanted to be promoted to a manager position. She wasn't willing to wait for her year-end review to find out how she was doing, so she asked to meet with her manager. Sophia asked her manager for feedback on what she was doing well, what she should improve, and what she needed to do to be promoted to a manager. His first response was vague—he said she was doing well and just needed to "step up." Wanting more clarity on what he meant, Sophia asked her manager for some examples of what "stepping up" would look like. He said that she was too quiet in meetings, and needed to speak up more and share her opinions. He also talked about a project that she had been asked to lead, and said that she needed to provide clearer direction to the team and delegate more. Once Sophia understood what her manager wanted to see, she made it a practice to speak up at every meeting she attended and volunteered to lead more meetings. She signed up for a New Managers class at her company to learn how to better lead a team and manage a project. And, she continued to ask her manager for feedback and for more opportunities to step up.

The following exercise will help you create a plan for developing your competence. To help you identify areas for development, you will be asked to assess your level of competence relative to your current position, as well as your level of competence relative to the position to which you aspire.

EXERCISE: COMPETENCE DEVELOPMENT

List the key areas of competence required by your *current position,* and rate your level of proficiency in each.

	Low				High
_____	1	2	3	4	5
_____	1	2	3	4	5
_____	1	2	3	4	5
_____	1	2	3	4	5
_____	1	2	3	4	5
_____	1	2	3	4	5

List the key areas of competence required by the *position to which you aspire*, and rate your level of proficiency in each.

	Low				High
_____	1	2	3	4	5
_____	1	2	3	4	5
_____	1	2	3	4	5
_____	1	2	3	4	5
_____	1	2	3	4	5
_____	1	2	3	4	5

What skills and abilities do you want to develop? Consider the following areas:

- Technical skills and expertise
- Communication skills
- Influence skills
- Leadership skills
- Political skills

What developmental experiences would you like to seek out?

What classes or training programs would you like to attend? What would you like to read? Who would you like to learn directly from?

Are you getting timely, specific, and candid feedback? If not, what can you do to get this kind of feedback?

Summary of Key Points

- A consistently high level of competence and performance makes a world of difference when it comes to long-term career success. Developing a deep level of expertise, continually mastering new skills, and learning from your experiences and feedback are essential.
- Doing good work is not enough. As you progress in your career, it is also critical to master communication, influence, leadership, and political skills.
- There are many ways to learn and develop your skills. You can learn from developmental experiences. You can learn from classes, training sessions, and reading. You can learn from informal conversations with others, and you can learn from feedback.
- If you're not receiving candid, constructive, and timely feedback, ask for it.
- Regardless of how you learn, leverage what you learn to benefit and add value to your work and your organization.

Personal Takeaways

Record your insights and respond to the questions on the following page.

What skills and abilities do you want to develop and hone?

What will you do to develop these skills and abilities?

Chapter 5

CREDIBILITY

Developing and sustaining credibility is an essential element of successfully managing your career. Your credibility is made up of your reputation and visibility. In other words, it is based on who knows you and what they believe about you.

Imagine that you are responsible for selecting a leader for a team that will be entrusted with an important project. A senior staff member informs you that there are two candidates of equal tenure and describes them as follows:

Description of Jennifer: "Jennifer is hard-working and smart. I've heard that she generally works through lunch, stays late during the week, and seems to work most weekends. She doesn't socialize with us or attend many company events, so I don't know her personally. She doesn't say much in meetings, although I see her taking notes. She's known as someone who is very reliable—you can always count on her to do whatever she's asked to do without errors and on time."

Description of Maria: "Maria is hard-working and smart. She'll stay late or work on weekends if it's necessary. Everyone loves Maria—she has great relationships internally and with clients. She's interested in learning about the department, the business, and the industry, and

49

goes out of her way to help other people. In meetings, Maria asks good questions and frequently offers up new ideas. She seems to like developing junior staff members, and I keep hearing about how they love working with her. She's not great with the details, but she gets the job done and often makes it even better."

Who would you pick to lead the team, and why? If you're like most people, you would ask Maria to lead the team, because it sounds like Maria has leadership skills, while it sounds like Jennifer does not. If Maria is selected to lead the team, she will be able to develop her leadership skills even further and will most likely strengthen her reputation as a leader. If Maria is selected, Jennifer will lose out on this opportunity to develop her leadership skills and will fall farther behind.

People make decisions about you based on their perceptions of you. Their perceptions are based on their firsthand experiences, their observations, and what they hear from other people. The decisions they make about you include whether to hire, mentor, give a plum assignment, offer a leadership position, or promote you.

Your reputation is the sum total of other people's perceptions. Notice that who you are on the inside, what you're thinking, and what you want are not part of this equation—*unless* you help other people understand these parts of you. You may not know what your reputation is right now, but other people do. It's important for you to be aware of your current reputation, so you can decide whether it serves you, and how you can strengthen and enhance it.

Your Current Reputation

The following exercise will help you assess your current reputation. Part 1 of the exercise is a self-assessment. While you may not know all the answers, respond to them as best you can. Part 2 asks you to get real feedback from people who you trust to be honest and candid with you, and who are well connected in your organization. Part 3 asks you to synthesize this information into a description of your current reputation. It may feel uncomfortable to take such a close look at yourself, but I encourage you to do this exercise.

Let me show you what Jennifer and Maria from our previous example learned after completing this exercise:

Jennifer: In responding to the questions in the self-assessment, Jennifer kept coming up with the same three concepts to describe herself—smart, reliable, and hard-working. She wasn't surprised by the feedback she gathered from others about her reputation. They told her she had a great reputation for getting the work done flawlessly, and they loved it when she was working on one of their projects because they never had to worry about it. Jennifer was ambitious and took this opportunity to ask about whether they saw her as a manager. Their first reaction was surprise; they didn't know she was interested in being a manager, and had never thought of her in this way. Jennifer realized that she had a reputation of being a worker bee and not a leader. This was Jennifer's first clue that she needed to do something different.

Maria: The three concepts that kept coming up for Maria in doing the self-assessment were high energy, people person, and big-picture oriented. When she asked others for feedback on her reputation, she heard things like leadership potential, connected in the organization, and good developer of people. Maria was ambitious and used these feedback conversations to let people know that she wanted to have more of an impact on the organization and wanted more management responsibilities. She realized that she had already developed a reputation as a leader, and wanted to continue to build on this reputation.

EXERCISE: CURRENT REPUTATION ASSESSMENT

PART I. Self-Assessment

Answer the following questions as best you can:

If I asked your manager to describe you in three words, what would those words be?

If I asked your peers to describe you in three words, what would those words be?

If I asked your direct reports to describe you in three words, what would those words be?

How would people complete these sentences? List only the things that you have heard *frequently* and *consistently*.

- "If you need someone to _____ _____, go see [you]."
- "If you need to know anything about _____ _____ go see [you]."

PART 2. Getting Feedback

Talk to two or three people who are well connected in your organization and whom you trust to give you candid feedback. Tell them that you are working on your career, and ask them for feedback on your current reputation. Listen to learn—manage any impulse you may have to argue, defend, explain, or tell the other person they are wrong. If you can, ask clarifying questions, such as "Can you give me an example of that?" or "Can you help me understand that better?" Then thank them for the information. Write down what you heard from them here.

PART 3. Your Reputation

Look at your self-assessment and the feedback you received. Summarize your current reputation here.

You now have a sense of your current reputation. The next step is to think about the reputation you *want* to have. Once you have done this, you can assess any differences between your current and desired reputation, and develop a plan to close the gap.

Your Personal Brand Is Your Desired Reputation

To move in the direction you want to go, you need to develop a reputation that reflects who you truly are and leads to opportunities that will help you move toward your career goals.

Think of your personal brand as your desired reputation and think of yourself as your personal brand manager. You can actively manage your personal brand—you can create it, communicate it, monitor its effectiveness, update it, and enhance it. Your objective is to have your *actual* reputation match your personal brand.

An effective personal brand is one that is authentic, differentiates you, and reflects the value you bring. It embodies what you can do, and more significantly, what you can do better than most of your peers. It encompasses your technical skills as well as your interpersonal and leadership skills. Your personal brand may have an aspirational component. It may include attributes that you do not now possess, as long as you are in the process of developing them.

As I am defining it, your personal brand is not your "elevator pitch." It is not a statement to be used to introduce yourself to others; rather, it is a statement to be used to ground yourself and guide your behaviors. It is an articulation of who you are and who you aspire to be at your very best. This is personal branding from the inside out.

The following exercise will walk you through a series of steps to create your personal brand. The examples below describe how Jennifer and Maria first articulated their brands, and then describe the personal brands they developed after they went through this exercise.

Jennifer: Jennifer started the exercise by saying that she wanted to be known as "someone who always did good work and was a good manager." After working through the exercise, she came up with the following personal brand: "High integrity and creative individual contributor/manager/leader with a deep understanding of company systems who can get complex projects done."

Maria: Maria began the exercise by saying she wanted to be known as "a great leader and someone who was fun to work with." After working through the exercise, she came up with the following personal brand: "Inspirational leader and strategic thinker who has strong technical and people skills, understands the business, delegates well, and can build and develop a team."

EXERCISE: CREATING YOUR PERSONAL BRAND

What do you want to be known for? Create a list of these attributes here.

Answer the following questions:

	yes	no
Are your personal brand attributes in alignment with your personal values, strengths, and interests?	☐	☐
If others believed you had these personal brand attributes, would they think of you for the opportunities that will help you achieve your short- and long-term goals?	☐	☐
Do your personal brand attributes differentiate you and showcase the unique value you bring to your organization?	☐	☐
Do your personal brand attributes reflect not only your technical competence, but also your communication, influence, and leadership skills?	☐	☐

If you answered "No" to any of these questions, refine your personal brand attributes so that you can answer this question in the affirmative. Write a final detailed description of your personal brand here.

Mind the Gap

You've now examined your current reputation and articulated your personal brand. Are there gaps—specific aspects of your personal brand that are not reflected in your current reputation? The following exercise will help you identify these areas, so you can address them strategically.

Once you identify the gap between your current reputation and your personal brand, you can develop your brand attributes and take steps to communicate your personal brand more effectively. If you've identified attributes that you do not currently possess, review Chapter 4 and put together a development plan for yourself. If you possess attributes that are not known or recognized, the following section will help you communicate these attributes more effectively.

If you find a wide gap between your current reputation and personal brand, you may need to take bold and memorable action to close the gap. If you determine that closing the gap is near impossible, refer to Chapter 11 and consider whether you need to move on.

EXERCISE: MIND THE GAP

Describe how your current reputation and your personal brand differ.

List the gap areas that reflect attributes that you *currently possess but that are not known or recognized* by others in your organization. These are attributes that need to be better communicated.

List the gap areas that reflect attributes that you *do not currently possess*. These are attributes that need to be developed and then communicated.

Communicating Your Personal Brand

Corporations not only spend a lot of time and effort on developing their brands, they also focus on developing powerful communication strategies to reach their target audience. Similarly, as your own personal brand manager, it is important for you to develop communication strategies to reach your target audience.

Here are examples of how James, Paula, and Reggie communicated their personal brands:

James: James, an executive, received feedback that there was a growing perception that he was not good at developing his direct reports. He sincerely cared about his people, and realized that he could do better. He wanted to be known as someone who was good at developing future leaders for the organization. James told his manager that developing his staff would be one of his top priorities going forward. He began to include a development discussion in each of his weekly one-on-one meetings with his direct reports, and he made an effort to give them more immediate feedback. He became more deliberate about taking them to meetings with senior executives. He also actively sponsored them for developmental opportunities and stretch assignments.

Paula: Paula was known as an individual contributor within her company, and yet she had held major leadership positions in her community for many years. She wanted to communicate to her organization that she was a leader, so she began sharing stories and lessons she had learned as a community leader. She also volunteered to head up a major event. Paula not only led the team organizing the event, she also took the stage as the opening speaker.

Reggie: Reggie worked at an accounting firm and aspired to become a partner. In order to be seen as a strong partner candidate, he stepped up his business development efforts and made it a practice to look for and pitch new business opportunities. He also noticed that all the partners in his office wore blazers despite the casual dress code. He was very comfortable with the look, and decided that he would wear blazers to the office as well.

James, Paula, and Reggie were not trying to be anyone other than who they genuinely were. They were just being more deliberate about their actions. They found ways to further develop their brand attributes and better communicate them. In my experience, the key to creating a powerful personal brand is to be more of who you genuinely are, and let other people see it.

There are four major ways personal brands are communicated—what you say and how you say it, what you do, your overall appearance or image, and what others say about you. Below is a description of each of these four communication methods, and after each one is an exercise that will help you think through what you can do to better communicate your personal brand.

What You Say and How You Say It

The messages you send are transmitted not only by your words, but also by your delivery and nonverbal behaviors. If your personal brand includes being an inspirational leader, then your words should reflect a leader's perspective *and* your delivery and posture should reflect confidence, passion, and connectedness with the group. If your personal brand includes being a trusted advisor, then your words should reflect your expertise and understanding of your client *and* your delivery and posture should reflect confidence and trustworthiness.

One of the most powerful ways to deliver a message and communicate your desired personal brand is through a story. Stories are memorable, easily repeated, and often become part of your reputation. They speak to your character as well as your actions and experience. Jennifer, from previous examples, wanted to be known as a leader. I asked Jennifer to tell me about her past leadership experiences. It was only then that she mentioned that she had been President of a 200-person student organization in college and had also been a chess champion. She had never shared stories about these experiences with anyone at the company. If she had, these stories would have helped others understand that Jennifer had the ability to lead people and think strategically. Stories such as these, when raised at the appropriate time and in the appropriate way, can be highly effective in communicating your desired personal brand.

How you say something also matters. Pay attention to your delivery—your voice, pitch, tone, volume, and pace. Think of some of the adjectives people use to describe other people's voices—"deep," "powerful," "seductive," "whiny," "annoying," etc. Think about how others would describe your voice. Similarly, pay attention to your nonverbal behaviors—your facial expressions, posture, nervous habits, eye contact, etc. Research suggests that in emotional conversations people will find more meaning in your delivery and nonverbal behaviors than in the words you speak. Therefore, it is critical to have congruence between your words, delivery, and nonverbal behaviors.

Your nonverbal behaviors are speaking even when you are not using any words. Your choice of where to sit at a meeting sends a message. People will notice whether you sit at the head of the table, somewhere in the middle, or off to the side. How you walk into a room sends a message. Walking confidently into a room will create a different impression of you than entering a room with uncertainty and tentativeness. Your resting facial expression will also send a message, even when none is intended. There are people whose resting facial expression suggests that they are angry or unwelcoming, while other people's resting facial expression suggests that they are open and approachable. Be aware of the messages you are sending even when you are not intending to send a message.

A quick word about social media. How you present yourself on social media communicates a message. Make sure that people who are viewing you on social media are receiving the message you intend to send, and are leaving with an impression of you that is consistent with your desired personal brand.

EXERCISE: WHAT YOU SAY AND HOW YOU SAY IT

For each of your desired brand attributes, think of a story that reflects that particular brand attribute. To help you quickly recall these stories, give each of them a title, and record that title here. Share these stories with others at the appropriate time.

Take a video of yourself telling one of your stories. Watch your video, assess your nonverbal behaviors, and notice your voice, pitch, tone, volume, and pace. Identify what you did well, and identify one or two behaviors that you can improve to be even more effective. Practice those one or two things, and record yourself again. For those of you who are afraid of this exercise, know that the most frequent response I've heard from people who watched themselves on video is "I'm not as bad as I thought I was." Make a note of what you learned in this exercise here.

What You Do

What you do at work and what you do outside of work become part of your reputation. When people hear that a colleague is working with senior management on a special project, they often assume that person is a well-respected high performer. When people hear that a colleague is training for a marathon, they often assume that person has a high degree of energy, discipline, and drive.

You can intentionally engage in activities that are consistent with and communicate your personal brand. Because your personal brand already reflects your values, strengths, and interests, engaging in these activities should feel authentic and not forced. Here are a few examples of activities that may help you communicate your personal brand:

- If your personal brand includes leadership, you can volunteer to lead a team, project, task force, or employee group. You can address strategic issues and help craft a vision for a project or team. You can help develop and mentor junior staff members.
- If your personal brand includes innovation, you can consistently offer up new ideas and suggestions, volunteer for cutting-edge projects, and affiliate yourself with departments charged with innovation.
- If your personal brand includes collaboration, you can seek out inter-departmental projects, build relationships across the organization, and look for ways to help people in other areas.
- If your personal brand includes being a subject matter expert, you can make presentations, write white papers, and hold training sessions. You can get involved in industry organizations or join advisory boards in your area of expertise.

EXERCISE: WHAT YOU DO

Identify activities that you currently engage in that are consistent with your desired personal brand. Consider how effectively they communicate your brand, and whether you want to continue, modify, or drop these activities.

Identify activities that you currently engage in that are inconsistent with your desired personal brand. Consider their impact on your reputation, and whether you want to continue, modify, or drop these activities.

What additional activities would you like to engage in that will help communicate your desired personal brand?

Image

People also develop perceptions of you based on your appearance or image. It may not be fair, but it happens. Think about your personal brand and think about your appearance. Is your appearance consistent with your desired personal brand? Consider the following:

- Attire—What does your clothing say about you? Notice how others you respect dress in your workplace. Notice how the senior people in your organization dress. A common piece of advice is to dress for the job you want, not the job you have.

- Hair—What does your hair say about you? I have gotten questions from clients about whether they should change their hairstyles, and some of my male clients have asked me what I think about facial hair. Here again, the question is: What image do you want to portray, and is your hairstyle or facial hair consistent with that image? This is a judgment call. You need to take into account your role, geography, and organizational culture to answer this question.

- Posture—What does your posture say about you? Think back to the Superman movies: Is your posture like Clark Kent's, or like Superman's? Clark Kent slouched, while Superman stood tall.

- Workspace—If someone walked by your workspace, what would their impression be of its occupant? Take a look. Is it neat and organized, or is it cluttered and chaotic? Be aware that other people may see this and describe you in the same way.

- Your team—If you manage a team, what does the behavior of your team say about you? If your team is sloppy and mistake-prone, others may infer the same is true of you. If your team is top-notch and high-performing, others may see this as a reflection of you.

Your image and appearance influence your reputation. Aligning your image with your personal brand will help you create the reputation you desire.

EXERCISE: IMAGE

If someone who didn't know you saw a picture of you taken in the midst of your workday, what would they think of you? What job, position, and responsibilities would they imagine the person in the picture had?

What can you do to better communicate your personal brand through your image?

What Others Say About You

Your colleagues, friends, and acquaintances play a role in communicating your personal brand and establishing your reputation. They are an important source of information about you. They are likely to tell others about their experiences with you, what they've heard you say, and what they've seen you do. This can work for you or against you. To make it work *for* you, you need to have a strong personal brand that is well communicated *and* you need strong, supportive relationships. Chapter 6 focuses on building these relationships.

Creating Visibility

To create meaningful visibility within your organization, your personal brand must be known by decision makers and their influencers. These are the people who are making critical decisions about you, including whether to promote you, or give you a plum assignment, more responsibility, or an opportunity for development and professional growth. Influencers are the people whom the decision makers rely on for information about you, your performance, and your potential.

There are many ways to increase your visibility. You might write a white paper, contribute to your corporate intranet, speak up at town halls and large events, propose and lead a new initiative within your organization, or take a visible leadership role. There are also daily practices that can increase your visibility—you can speak up in meetings, share your thoughts and ideas, volunteer for assignments, and actively participate in events and gatherings. Remember that just as your personal brand is authentic, the actions you take to increase your visibility must also be authentic.

Take a look at how Martin, Justin, and Magda increased their visibility in their organizations:

Martin: The CEO of Martin's company periodically held gatherings for groups of employees where she shared her thinking and invited questions. Martin, realizing how important visibility was, attended one of these gatherings and made a point of asking a question about a critical issue facing the business. The CEO was so impressed with the question that she made a point of talking to Martin after the session.

Justin: Justin, a single father, noticed that while his company had groups and events for working mothers, it did not have similar groups or events for working fathers. After speaking to a few senior men who were enthusiastic about the idea, Justin started the first-ever fathers group at his organization. He led the first meeting, which was well attended, and was recognized for his effort by several senior executives.

Magda: Magda had just completed her company's six-month initial training program and been placed on a permanent team. She was young, but she already knew she was interested in a leadership position. Magda had developed a great relationship with the manager of her training program and volunteered to help with the new class of trainees. She organized informal lunches with her peers to share information and support each other. Magda also actively participated in department and company events, and volunteered to help and do more at every opportunity.

EXERCISE: CREATING VISIBILITY

Who are the decision makers and key influencers who can impact your career? If you don't know who they are, how can you find out?

What can you do to raise your visibility and communicate your personal brand to them?

Continually monitor your reputation and manage your personal brand. What you do after work or on weekends may become part of your reputation. How you act at a holiday party may become part of your reputation. What you say "off the record" may become part of your reputation. I have known people who, despite being major contributors at work, torpedoed their careers because of behaviors that were deemed to be inconsistent with their company's values and ethics. Be vigilant and protect your reputation.

Developing and sustaining credibility is an essential element of successfully managing your career. Understand your current reputation and be thoughtful about what you need to do to develop a reputation that reflects who you really are and helps you reach your career goals. Actively manage your personal brand. Create it, communicate it, monitor its effectiveness, update, and enhance it. Your personal brand can help you lead your way.

Summary of Key Points

- Developing and sustaining credibility is an essential element of successfully managing your career. Your credibility is made up of your reputation and visibility. In other words, it is based on who knows you and what they believe about you.
- People make decisions about you based on your reputation.
- Your personal brand is your *desired* reputation. An effective personal brand is one that is authentic, differentiates you, and reflects the value you bring to your organization. Develop a reputation that reflects who you are and leads to opportunities that will help you achieve your career goals.
- You are your own personal brand manager. Create, communicate, monitor, update, and enhance your personal brand.
- There are four major ways personal brands are communicated—what you say and how you say it, what you do, your overall appearance or image, and what others say about you.

- Build your visibility and communicate your personal brand to decision makers and their influencers.
- Continually monitor your reputation and manage your personal brand.

Personal Takeaways

Record your insights and respond to the questions on the following page.

What is your personal brand; i.e., your desired reputation?

What personal brand attributes do you want to develop? What will you do to develop them?

What personal brand attributes do you want to better communicate? What will you do to better communicate them?

With whom do you want to increase your visibility? What will you do to increase your visibility?

Chapter 6

- ✤

RELATIONSHIPS

Your relationships are key to helping you lead your way. Having relationships across your organization with people at different levels and with diverse backgrounds opens doors not only to learning and development, but to critical opportunities for you to grow and be recognized. When you meet these opportunities with high performance, your competence, credibility, and confidence become even stronger and you are well on your way to moving your career forward.

Meet Charles and some of the people in his relationship network:

Charles and Sam started working at the company on the same day. They've become friends and often have lunch together. If one hears about anything that's happening in the organization that might impact the other, or hears of an opportunity that the other might be interested in, he makes sure the other person knows about it. They have a trusting relationship in which information flows.

Charles and Anika met on the job and instantly hit it off. They share the same background and a common way of looking at the world, and have overcome similar challenges. If Charles is having a bad day, the first person he calls is Anika. She is always supportive and encouraging, and reminds him of how good he is at what he does. Charles does the same for Anika. They have a supportive friendship.

Charles met Nancy through a training program he attended. Charles was so impressed with Nancy that he asked to meet with her to learn more about her background and career path. Over time, their relationship deepened, and Charles now seeks out Nancy's advice, not only on his career, but also on working with other parts of the organization and handling sticky situations. Charles is very appreciative of Nancy's time and counsel, and goes out of his way to help her out in any way he can. Nancy is acting as a mentor.

Michael has major responsibilities in the division where Charles works, and is highly influential. Michael doesn't interact with Charles much, but is impressed by what he's heard about Charles's initiative and high performance, and has noticed that he always seems eager to do more. When Michael is selecting people for a high-profile task force, he puts Charles on the list. Michael is acting as a sponsor.

There are many kinds of relationships. At their deepest, relationships are trusting, caring connections between two individuals. They are mutually beneficial—both parties give and both parties benefit. They can also take the form of acquaintanceships in which two people know each other but do not have a close personal connection. There may be some transfer of value in acquaintanceships, but it does not always exist and, when it does, it tends to be episodic and may be one-way.

Having strong relationships has many benefits, including helping you perform your job at a higher level. You tend to have better information, you know whom to call to get things done, and you have people who will help you out when you need a favor.

Having strong relationships helps you manage your career. Having people who can serve as a reality check or sounding board can be invaluable when you have critical career decisions to make. Having diverse relationships gives you multiple role models and perspectives to learn from, and also gives you access to different information flows. Strong relationships with key people often lead to being considered for opportunities or job openings, even before positions are posted.

Having strong relationships can give you much-needed emotional support and encouragement. Careers tend to have high and low points, and having people to talk to when you need a boost can make a big difference in your experience and your ability to be resilient.

Having strong relationships with well-respected people also has a compounding effect. Trust is transferable through relationships. If I know and respect someone who trusts you, then I will trust you as well, unless or until you prove undeserving of my trust. Esteem is also transferable through relationships. If I know and respect someone who holds you in high esteem, then I will assume that you are deserving of high esteem, unless or until you prove me wrong.

Charles's relationship network includes people who share information, support and care about him, provide advice, and create opportunities for him to shine. The following sections focus on two kinds of relationships that deserve special attention—mentors and sponsors. One person may serve both roles; but I distinguish them because that is not always the case.

Mentors

Mentors serve a critical career function. Mentors give wise counsel and advice, and oftentimes needed encouragement and support. Mentors can reside at any level within or outside of your organization. It doesn't matter whether a mentor has power in your organization—all that matters is that they can support your development.

It is important to build multiple and diverse mentoring relationships. Having the perspectives of people with different backgrounds and experiences can be invaluable in expanding your thinking and helping you make the best decisions.

I know people who have met a senior person for the first time and immediately asked them to be their mentor. This approach sometimes works. I also know senior people who reject this approach, especially when they have no pre-existing relationship with the person seeking mentorship. I generally advise my clients to take the more organic approach of first establishing a relationship, and then engaging in mentoring conversations with the other person.

With either approach, the first step is to identify people you want to learn from. Once you identify them, look for opportunities to engage in deeper conversations. Find areas of commonality to establish rapport, and be sincerely interested in learning about and from them. Ask for their advice on career-related issues, and be appreciative. Let them know when you have taken their advice, and what the outcome was. Find ways to give back to them—the most productive and long-lasting mentoring relationships are two-way.

Sponsors

In contrast to a mentor, a sponsor needs to have some power. Sponsors use their social and political capital to further your career. They may give you exposure at higher levels in the organization, recommend and support you for opportunities and stretch assignments, and provide protection when needed. While your relationship with a mentor entails direct interaction, this may not be true of a sponsor. A sponsor may just see or hear about you and act, and you may never know that there was an invisible hand behind an opportunity you were given unless you ask. You can develop mentors, or actively engage in mentoring conversations, but you must *attract* sponsors.

You attract sponsors by doing everything I've been talking about—performing at a consistently high level, having a strong, well-known personal brand that is valued by the organization, and being known by decision makers and influencers. If a senior person takes an interest in you, take notice, and nurture that relationship. Always be prepared to answer the question "What would you like to do here at the company?" If a senior person asks you this question, it is likely that they are interested in you and your career, and may be considering sponsoring you.

You might be wondering why someone would put the time and effort into sponsoring or mentoring others. Mentors and sponsors do benefit from these relationships when they are two-way. In ongoing, successful mentoring relationships, the mentee helps the mentor in any way he or she can, shares information, and shows appreciation and respect. In long-term sponsor relationships, the protégé makes the sponsor look good, contributes to the business with sustained, visible high performance, shows appreciation and loyalty, and does whatever they can to help their sponsor.

Relationship Network Assessment

You can proactively develop and manage your relationships. You can deepen your current relationships and form new ones, and you can do this strategically and authentically.

Your relationship network is the sum total of your relationships. A healthy and robust network includes relationships that span an organization and extend outside of the organization. It has a high percentage of deep, significant relationships and includes demographic diversity, as well as diversity of experience, thought, and perspective.

The process of building relationships is sometimes referred to as "networking." I have met many people who have a negative reaction to the term "networking"—to them, it connotes being inauthentic, making small talk, and interacting in a superficial manner solely for selfish purposes. For me, networking is about *building authentic two-way relationships*. Because of how important this is, I address some of the most common challenges that hold people back from networking later in this chapter and propose ways to overcome them.

The following exercise will lead you through a process to analyze your current relationships, pinpoint the gaps in your network, and help you identify people with whom you would like to build or deepen your relationship.

EXERCISE: RELATIONSHIP NETWORK ASSESSMENT

PART I. Think about the people with whom you currently have a relationship.

List the names of people who are important sources of information about your job, organization, and/or career.

List the names of your mentors; i.e., people who provide you with career advice, feedback, and encouragement. They may be at any level—senior to you, peers, or junior to you.

List the names of your sponsors; i.e., people who use their power and influence to provide you with opportunities for development and advancement.

List the names of people who are in your support group; i.e., people who provide you with emotional support around work experiences and issues.

PART 2. Transfer the names of each person you listed in Part 1 into the applicable category below. After each name, put the letter(s) describing the nature of the relationship: Information (I), Mentorship (M), Sponsorship (S), or Support (Sup). One relationship may have multiple attributes.

	Within your company and department	Within your company and outside of your department	Outside of your company
Senior to you			
Your peer			
Junior to you			

PART 3. Look for the gaps in your relationship network and how you can fill these gaps.

Consider the gaps in your relationship network in terms of function or placement on the grid. Also consider how diverse your relationship network is in terms of gender, ethnicity, and other demographic characteristics, as well as diversity of perspectives, experiences, and thought. Describe the gaps in your relationship network here:

List the names of people you would like to add to your relationship network. If you identify a gap and don't know anyone who can fill it, ask people you know for suggestions.

Building Relationships

Think back to a relationship that developed effortlessly. There was proximity and you probably felt a natural affinity with that person—you liked each other, it was easy to connect, and you wanted to spend more time together. This is not always the case in the workplace. You will most likely need or want to build relationships with people with whom you don't normally interact or feel the same kind of natural affinity.

Here are some tips for intentionally building a relationship where proximity and natural affinity are not the starting point:

- **Find and create opportunities to interact**—If you would not normally cross paths with this person, find ways to interact. Schedule a meeting, lunch, or coffee with them, or attend meetings or events where the other person is present and make a point of talking with them. I have heard of people who have signed up for projects in order to work with a particular individual, gotten involved in activities that the other person was involved in, or made a point to come into the office early to interact with someone who was known to routinely arrive early to the office.

- **Engage**—After you find or create the opportunity to interact, engage the other person in conversation. Be genuinely interested in the other person. Listen and ask questions. Share relevant information about yourself.

- **Find and build on commonalities**—As you listen to what the other person is saying, ask more questions, and look for and highlight areas of commonality.

- **Pick up on signals and clues**—Much of communication happens at a nonverbal level; e.g., a sigh or a wink or a roll of the eyes. Similarly, a lot of information is communicated through quick side comments, like "What a day" or "I'm exhausted." Pick up on these signals and ask about them. You just might take the conversation to a deeper level.

- **Establish rapport**—Focus on building a trusting relationship. Try not to ask for a favor up front without investing in building a relationship first.
- **Give generously and without expectation of getting anything in return**—Whenever you can help someone, do it. People appreciate your help and tend to want to pay it back. If you ever need a favor, these same people will most likely want to help you.
- **Follow up**—One conversation does not make a relationship. Real relationships happen over time. At the end of a conversation, think about how you can continue the dialogue. There may be information you can send to this person to follow up on the conversation. There may be topics you want to ask about the next time you talk. Jot down a few notes and review them before your next conversation. This can be very helpful, especially with people you don't see very often.

In addition to being strategic about building relationships, I encourage you to capitalize on spontaneous opportunities to build relationships. If you find yourself next to someone you don't know at a meeting or event, introduce yourself and engage with them. They are a potential friend, and may become a client, partner, boss, or employee in the future.

Building Your Relationship Network

Let's go back to Charles, from earlier in this chapter. Charles made building relationships look easy. Let's examine what he actually did.

Charles: Charles liked people, enjoyed interacting with them, and derived a lot of energy from these interactions. When he went to the coffee station on his floor, he greeted whoever was there. Sometimes, both he and the other person were looking for a break, and so what could have been a brief greeting became a longer conversation. When a new person joined the department, he introduced himself, tried to learn more about them, and offered to help them out. He enjoyed going to company events where he was able to see friends and meet interesting new people. Everyone worked hard at his company, so Charles was always respectful of other people's time. Charles was also aware of who the senior people were in his company. He made a special effort to talk with them whenever he had the opportunity. At events, before approaching someone he hadn't met before, he would quickly think about how he would introduce himself, what questions he might ask, and what information he wanted to share.

While there are people like Charles who seem to be made for networking, there are others like Jennifer (from the previous chapter) who find networking hard.

Here is Jennifer's story:

Jennifer: "I've never been good at networking. It's hard for me to start up a conversation with someone I don't know. It feels fake, or it feels like I'm just trying to get to know them so they can help me. I hate small talk, and I usually feel like I don't have anything in common with the other person. There is someone I'd like to get to know better, but she works remotely so I never see her. I'm horrible at big social events—I always feel awkward, so I just don't go."

Jennifer is describing some of the most common challenges faced by people who struggle with networking. Here are some suggestions on how to overcome these challenges:

- **When it feels fake**—When it feels fake or inauthentic to reach out to another person, it's often because you just don't want to talk with them. Try to identify the reason or belief beneath this reluctance to engage with them. If you determine that your reason is valid, don't engage. If, on the other hand, you question the validity of your reason or belief, refer to Chapter 9 on Limiting Beliefs for guidance. One potential strategy is to shift your mindset. Instead of thinking, "I don't want to talk to this person," try adopting a mindset that is more conducive to a positive interaction, perhaps something as simple as "It will be fun to talk to this person," "I'm going to learn something valuable by talking to this person," or "There's something I can help this person out with." Shifting your mindset may help you have a positive interaction with this person that you might not otherwise have had.

- **When it feels self-serving**—If you think of networking as self-serving behavior where people are only focused on what the other person can do for them, then you may very well shy away from it. Remember that the best relationships are mutually beneficial. Be interested in helping the other person out and being of value to them. Take that spirit into every interaction with others and you will enrich the experience for both of you.

- **Difficulty with small talk**—Some people say that they don't like small talk. Small talk assumes a dialogue about meaningless things. If that's what it is, then no one enjoys small talk. I suggest that instead of engaging in small talk, you engage in meaningful talk. Be curious and use this as an opportunity to learn. Ask questions about the other person's background, experiences, job, challenges, areas of expertise, or interests. And then share relevant information about yourself.

- **Feeling different from others**—When you feel different from others in your organization, it can be very difficult to build relationships. Feeling different can happen based on many dimensions, including differing interests, backgrounds, or outlooks. If this is how you feel, it is important to try to find commonalities, often at a deeper level. There may be commonalities around values, family situations, life stages, or perhaps a fondness for certain foods, books, or vacation sites. You may need to work a little harder in these situations. I address this more in Chapter 8.

- **Working virtually**—Relationships are even more challenging to establish when you work in different locations. The steps are the same, but you need to be more deliberate. Try to find time on a call to talk more personally, perhaps at the beginning or end of the call. Jot down notes about the events and activities the other person is engaged in, and make a point of asking about them on the next call. Send a personal note when appropriate. If you're always talking to someone over the phone, look for opportunities to meet in person whenever you are in the same vicinity. Consider using video conferencing technology. I had a client in London who, on our first video conference call, carried his laptop around, gave me a tour of his office, and introduced me to his teammates. It was a great way to connect with people 3,500 miles away.

- **Conferences and large events**—I believe that it is better to collect a few quality relationships than 100 business cards from people who you don't remember and who don't remember you. Here are some tips for developing higher-quality relationships at large events: Before the event, find out who is attending, select one or a few that you want to focus on, and develop a strategy to meet them. Decide how you will introduce yourself. Find out more about the other person/people before the event, and craft a compelling start to the conversation that will grab their attention and make them want to talk with you. If you don't know a lot about them, ask questions, and share information that relates to their interests. In addition, make a point of talking to the people around you. Sit next to people you don't know, and talk to them during breaks. Start a conversation in the buffet line while you're getting your food and, if you're interested in the other person, suggest you sit together to continue the conversation. If you're interested in continuing the conversation after the event, exchange contact information and make plans to meet again. Have a purpose and a topic for your next meeting.

Some people build relationships and then never ask for help or advice. They may feel that they need to do things on their own, or feel uncomfortable asking. The truth is that asking for help or advice can sometimes deepen a relationship. It makes the other person feel valued and important, and gives them the opportunity to return a favor or feel good about themselves because they helped someone they care about.

If reaching out to people takes you outside of your comfort zone, you can expect to feel some trepidation. If, however, you encounter people who make you uncomfortable because of issues related to personal boundaries or safety, then stop and assess the situation. Seek out the help of friends and mentors and decide how to deal with the situation.

Maintaining, Nurturing, and Expanding Your Relationship Network

Relationships change and develop over time. People leave and new people come onto the scene. You may outgrow your mentor. Sponsors may move on, get distracted, change their agenda, or lose their power. Friends may grow apart. You and your needs may change. I've met too many people who tell me that they "used to have a great mentor or sponsor," and then go on to say that their mentor or sponsor left the company five years ago and no one had taken their place.

Keep your relationship network current and robust so that you can continue to benefit from it and be a benefit to it. Periodically review and update your Relationship Network Exercise. Reassess your gaps, and be strategic and deliberate in filling those gaps. The time and effort you put into this is an investment in your long-term career success.

Summary of Key Points

- Your relationships are key to helping you lead your way. Having relationships across your organization with people at different levels and with diverse backgrounds opens doors not only to learning and development, but to critical opportunities for you to grow and be recognized.
- At their deepest, relationships are trusting and caring connections between two individuals that are mutually beneficial.
- Relationships can serve several career purposes, including information transference, mentoring, sponsorship, and support.
- Mentors give wise counsel and advice, and oftentimes encouragement and support. Sponsors are people in positions of power who can open doors and provide opportunities for development and advancement.
- Build relationships strategically. The first step is to identify people you want to develop relationships with and then find or create opportunities to interact. Engage, find, and build on commonalities, establish rapport, and give generously without expectation of getting anything in return. Create an ongoing dialogue by following up.
- Capitalize on spontaneous opportunities to build relationships. Take advantage of chance encounters.
- Relationships change and develop. Continually nurture, maintain, and expand your relationship network throughout your career.

Personal Takeaways

Record your insights and respond to the questions on the following page.

With whom do you want to build or deepen relationships?

What will you do to build or deepen these relationships?

Chapter 7

CONFIDENCE

Having confidence means that you have an unshakable faith in yourself. You know what you are capable of, and you believe that you can succeed. I am not talking about hubris or an overinflated sense of self. I am talking about the confidence that comes from knowing who you are and what you can do.

When you have confidence, you are more likely to speak up and be heard. You are more likely to take on stretch assignments. When faced with challenges or negative experiences, you are more likely to be resilient and persevere. And, if you act with confidence, others are more likely to have confidence in you.

Here is an example of stepping up with confidence, followed by an example of not doing so:

Katherine: Katherine is one of the leaders of her Employee Resource Group. She had the idea of creating her company's first-ever ERG Professional Development Conference. She asked the leaders of the other ERGs in her company whether their groups would like to co-sponsor the event. She invited executives to attend and speak, and on the day of the event she stepped to the podium in the role of Master of Ceremonies. She had never done anything of this magnitude before, but she had experienced a lot of success in her role at the company, and she knew she could do it. Her confidence and enthusiasm energized the group and led to a highly successful event.

Margaret: Margaret walks into meetings, head slightly lowered, takes the seat farthest away from the person leading the meeting, opens her notebook, and gets ready to take notes. She is known as technically excellent, and has always shied away from being in the spotlight. Margaret explains, "My manager keeps wanting me to do more and talks about promoting me. I don't know why. I'm not that good. There are so many other people who are better than me."

Katherine is full of confidence. She approaches her work with an "I can do it" attitude, and she steps boldly into new projects and roles. Margaret is lacking confidence at this stage in her career. She believes that she is "not that good," and she holds back from speaking up and taking on more responsibility. She discounts and questions the positive feedback she receives from her manager. And yet, there must be more to the story for her manager to want to promote her. How can Margaret develop the confidence to be able to take advantage of the opportunities her manager wants to give her? How can you develop the confidence you need to take advantage of your opportunities?

First of all, you need to believe that you can develop confidence—that it isn't only something people are born with. Think about confidence as something that you can get better at. Focus on things that are under your control. There are some factors impacting confidence that are beyond our control. And some of these factors may require a deeper dive than what I can provide in this book. If you are facing some of these deeper issues, I encourage you to seek out the help you need to address them.

Generally, people develop confidence from experiencing successes and overcoming challenges. They develop confidence from the encouragement, support, and championing they receive from other people. And they develop confidence from seeing people like themselves succeed, which leads to a sense that "If they can do it, so can I."

The exercise on the following page will guide you through a series of questions designed to help you remember and identify some of your sources of confidence. If you are someone who hasn't realized—or has forgotten—how good you really are, consider asking someone who knows you well to help you answer these questions. Let these questions lead your way to a place of greater confidence.

EXERCISE: CONFIDENCE ASSESSMENT

What are you really good at?

What do you enjoy doing?

What do you consider your greatest accomplishment(s) in your career?

What do you consider your greatest accomplishment(s) in your personal life?

Describe an experience when you overcame an obstacle or challenge through perseverance and hard work.

Describe an instance when you saw someone else succeed and thought, "If they can do it, I can do it."

What do your biggest supporters say about you?

When Margaret did this exercise, this is what she discovered:

Margaret: "I was really surprised by the exercise. I realized I enjoy talking to people. I volunteer in a tutoring program on weekends. At first it was hard, but now I love it. I'm really good at teaching, and I want to do more of it. About a year ago, my manager told me that they wanted to give me a few people to manage, and I kind of freaked out. But, if I think of it as an opportunity to teach, I might be able to do it. Recently, my manager nominated me for our company's high-potential leadership program. Maybe it's because I completed an assignment that no one else could. It saved the company a lot of money...I guess I'm not that bad."

Every career has its ups and downs. If you hit a point in your career where your confidence falters, come back to this exercise. Remind yourself of how much you've accomplished, how you've overcome challenges in the past, and how much others have believed in you.

Increasing Your Confidence

If you are looking for ways to increase your confidence even further, here are some tips:

- Surround yourself with positive, supportive people who believe in you and encourage you. Create an informal or formal group of supporters who actively help each other achieve their goals. In one of my programs, four women bonded and formed a deep friendship that extended from their professional to their personal lives. Although one took a job with another company, they still text each other daily, share information, ask for help, and support each other in their careers. In another program I facilitated, the participants decided on their own to form small support groups.

Many of these groups still meet, often virtually, to continue to support and encourage each other. The people involved in these support groups share stories about how much their group has helped them persevere in times of challenge, encouraged them in times of uncertainty, and celebrated with them in times of success. Here is Jackie's story:

> **Jackie:** "Thank goodness for friends. I have a tendency to think I'm not good enough. I had an opportunity to interview for a new position, and I wasn't sure about going for it. I talked to some friends, and they held up a mirror for me and reminded me of what I had done in the past. They said, 'You're good. What's the problem?' It's because of them that I went after the job and I got it."

- Look for opportunities to learn, grow, and experience success. Find low-risk venues to practice and hone your skills. Here is how Sebastian did it:

> **Sebastian:** "I used to be really afraid of public speaking and I avoided it at all costs. That is, until I participated in a program where I had the opportunity to prepare a story and present it in front of the group. After I finished presenting my story, I was overwhelmed by the applause and the compliments I received from the group. It took just that one positive experience to help me realize that I was good at making presentations, and now I volunteer for them whenever I can."

- Set a small goal in a specific area and achieve it; then continue to set small goals and achieve them. Each success will give you more confidence to undertake the next goal. Henry tells us how he went about this:

Henry: "I always thought that people didn't want to talk to me, so I kept to myself. I avoided company events and get-togethers whenever I could. After I realized that this was hurting my career, I decided I had to step out of my comfort zone and make an effort. I started just saying 'hi' to people, then I started asking if they needed help with something, and then when I felt a little more comfortable, I began having longer conversations. My confidence grew as I discovered that people were happy to talk with me."

- Look broadly for role models. These are people you can relate to in some way who have succeeded at what you want to do. I've met people who look to the upper echelons of their organizations and say, "I don't see anyone like me. I can't succeed here." I have also met people who have said, "I don't see anyone like me, and I can be the first." If the first reaction resonates with you, then I encourage you to look more broadly. Look at other areas of your organization, or look outside of your organization. Look for role models beyond those who are visibly like you—perhaps there is someone who shares the same academic background, skill set, experiences, values, or outlook. You may find your inspiration in unexpected places. Jorge provides an example of that.

Jorge: "I used to question whether, as a Hispanic man, I could reach a leadership position in my organization. There wasn't anyone who looked like me in my office and in my area. I started looking around and got to know some senior men who, while not Hispanic, I could relate to. One of them went to my college, and another was married to a Colombian woman. I reached out to them to ask about their experiences, and it helped me feel like I had a chance. One of the reasons I wanted to be an executive was so that I could be a role model for younger Hispanics. I want them to know that if I can make it, they can too."

- Adopt a positive presumption in your interactions with others. It will help you interpret their behavior in the best light and allow you to act most constructively. Gina gives us some insight:

> **Gina:** "I've always believed that people wanted to help me. I once worked with this senior guy who had a reputation for being difficult and demanding. Other people had a lot of trouble with him, but I never did. I knew he just wanted to help me be better, so I listened to him and tried to learn everything I could from him. He ended up being one of my biggest supporters."

If you are in a toxic environment that is eroding or has eroded your confidence, you may need to extricate yourself. There is more on this in Chapter 11. Additionally, there are other limiting beliefs that may feel like a lack of confidence. These are addressed in Chapter 9.

Confidence can be developed. Use the Confidence Assessment Exercise to help you understand where your confidence comes from. Use the tips above to nurture and build your confidence as you develop in your career. If there are deeper issues impacting your confidence, seek out the appropriate kind of counseling to address these issues.

Summary of Key Points

- Confidence is a deep belief in yourself, your capabilities, and your ability to succeed.
- Having a high degree of confidence helps you engage in more challenging and visible activities, increases your resilience and ability to

recover from negative experiences, and helps you persevere in the face of challenging situations.

- When you have confidence, other people are more likely to have confidence in you.
- Confidence comes from experiencing successes, overcoming challenges, and having the encouragement of others who believe in you. It can also come from seeing people like yourself succeed.
- Tips for increasing your confidence:
  - ▶ Surround yourself with positive, supportive people who believe in you and encourage you.
  - ▶ Look for opportunities to learn skills, develop strengths, and experience success.
  - ▶ Set a small goal in a specific area and achieve it; then, continue to set small goals and achieve them.
  - ▶ Look broadly for role models.
  - ▶ Adopt a positive presumption in your interactions with others.
- If there are deeper issues impacting your confidence, seek out the appropriate kind of counseling to address these issues.

Personal Takeaways

Record your insights and respond to the questions on the following page.

How would you describe your confidence level as it pertains to important aspects of your job?

What can you do to increase and/or maintain your confidence?

Chapter 8

- -

CHALLENGES FOR
UNDERREPRESENTED GROUPS

Thus far, I have been focusing on what everyone can do to prepare to be luckier in their careers. And, if you fit in with your organizational culture and current leadership, that may be sufficient. If, however, you feel like you don't fit in with your organizational culture or leadership and you are part of a group that is underrepresented in your organization, then you may be faced with some additional challenges. This may apply to women and people of color, as well as to those who feel different because of their sexual orientation, educational or socioeconomic background, or a number of other dimensions. If you feel this way, this chapter is for you.

These additional challenges fall into three general areas—facing stereotypes and bias, difficulty establishing relationships, and being overlooked for opportunities. While these challenges can stall or derail careers, there are things you can do to address and overcome them.

First of all, focus on what you *can* control, and follow the guidance set forth in this book. In addition to the strategies described in this chapter, make sure you select work and an organization that align with your values, strengths, and interests, and strategically and proactively develop your competence, credibility, confidence, and relationships.

I believe that organizations and leaders share responsibility for addressing these challenges, but that is a topic for another book. It takes time for organizations to change, and I have found that my clients are not willing to put their careers on hold to wait for that change. They want to act, and act now.

This chapter describes strategies and tips to address the additional organizational challenges you may face.

Facing Stereotypes and Bias

Stereotypes and bias exist. People have preconceived opinions and beliefs about individuals or groups, which can be positive or negative. These biases can impact the way people are recruited, developed, evaluated, and promoted. They can impact the way projects and clients are assigned, the way information is shared, and the way opportunities are distributed. Some people may benefit from these biases; others suffer negative consequences.

The impact of bias based on stereotypes is often compounded by the cognitive biases we are all subject to. For example, there is confirmation bias—people tend to take in the data that confirms their assumptions and to disregard data that is counter to their assumptions. There is affinity or in-group bias—people tend to like people like themselves and view them in a favorable light. There is the halo effect—when people see one positive characteristic in someone, they tend to impute other positive characteristics to them. And there is the horns effect—when people see one negative characteristic in someone, they tend to impute other negative characteristics to them.

Some of these biases and stereotypes are conscious and known. Others are held by individuals without any conscious awareness. Unconscious biases can be particularly insidious, because they can cause the most well-intentioned person to act in a way which has an unintended negative impact.

It is sometimes difficult to identify bias as the root or contributing factor in an interaction or experience. If you consistently perform at a high level and are never given the opportunity to further develop your skills, you may wonder if bias is at play. If you are encouraged to follow a career path counter to your interests but in line with stereotypes, you may wonder if bias is at play. If your manager seems surprised when you act in ways that run counter to stereotypes, you may wonder if bias is at play. You may start to doubt yourself or the other person, and this feeling may erode your self-confidence and your trust in the relationship. When you are the recipient of multiple interactions like this, it adds up, and you may end up feeling demoralized and demotivated. If this sounds like you, go back and review Chapter 7. Revisit the Confidence Assessment Exercise, reground yourself in your strengths and achievements, and remind yourself how good you are.

If you find yourself in a situation where you suspect your manager or someone else you work with is biased, there are things you can do. Consider the following:

- **Analyze the situation and ask for help from others.** If you suspect that prejudice and bias may be at play, analyze the situation. Reach out to your friends and mentors and ask them for a reality check. Describe your experience, and ask for their perspective and advice. They may provide you with knowledge or insights that will help you better understand the situation.

- **Decide what kind of relationship you want to have with this person.** Consider how important this person is to your work and your career, and how frequently you need to interact with them. Decide how much effort you want to put into nurturing this relationship. You may decide to invest time and effort, or you may decide to walk away. If you're considering making a move, consult Chapter 11 for guidance.

- **Adopt an attitude that allows you to deal constructively with the other person.** Racism, sexism, and other forms of prejudice can exist in the workplace, and it's important not to ignore them. At the same time, if you can adopt an attitude that allows you to deal constructively with the other person, you may be able to foster more positive interactions. Consider whether there may be reasons other than prejudice or bias for the person's behaviors. Perhaps the other person is inexperienced, uninformed, or insecure; or is under intense pressure to get the job done; or is dealing with a major life event. Try to adopt an attitude that allows you to see them as a whole person and to interact with them more constructively.

- **If possible, develop your relationship.** Build a personal relationship with them if you can. Ask them out for coffee or lunch. Find out more about them personally. Share more about yourself.

- **Decide whether and how to address the behavior.** Decide whether you want to have a conversation with the other person about the offending behavior. Assess the potential benefits and risks of raising the issue with them. Seek out the advice of mentors to decide whether, when, and how to have the conversation. Consider whether the conversation is best had by you or by someone else on your behalf. Be clear about your objectives for this conversation and your desired outcome.

- **Competence, Credibility, Confidence, Relationships.** Pay attention to everything covered in Chapters 2–7. When your work is in alignment with your values, strengths, and interests and you have clear goals, you are more likely to have the drive and conviction to face and overcome challenges rooted in bias. When you have a high level of competence, it is harder for others to question your value to the organization. With an authentic and powerful personal brand and visibility, you are more likely to be noticed and receive mentoring, sponsorship, and protection. And with a broad network of relationships, you have multiple people speaking up for you, representing you, and helping to minimize the potentially negative impact of prejudice and bias.

- **As a preemptive strategy, actively work to make a great first impression in all your interactions.** First impressions are formed quickly and will influence your future interactions. Be diligent about making a positive first impression. Let your competence shine through. Be thoughtful about your appearance, your message, and your introduction. Be aware of stereotypes. Make sure your first impression reflects your personal brand and who you really are.

Here is an example of how bias and stereotypes impacted Eileen's ability to develop in her career:

Eileen: Eileen was the only Asian American in her department. She worked hard and excelled at her work. When a new manager came in to lead her department, she often volunteered to take on leadership roles and make presentations, but her new manager always found ways to say no. She wasn't happy about it, and despite wondering whether being Asian had anything to do with her manager's reluctance to give her these opportunities, she never spoke up. Her suspicion was confirmed a year later, after this manager left the company. It was then that she heard that he used to say, "I wish I had a department full of Asians, because they are such great workhorses." Eileen knew that one of the stereotypes about Asians was that they were "workhorses"—great at executing the work, but not leadership material. Knowing that she was the only Asian American in her department, Eileen could only attribute her lack of professional development that year to her manager's bias.

Eileen could have done many things during the year she worked with this manager to change her experience. A great starting point would have been to invest in building a quality relationship with him. Eileen could have found or created opportunities to interact on a personal level, learned more about him, and shared more about herself. She could have told him about her career and leadership aspirations, and asked for his help in developing her leadership skills. While she may have suspected that her manager was biased, it would have been important for Eileen to find a constructive mindset to adopt—perhaps the belief that her manager wasn't aware of how much she was capable of, or that he might be overwhelmed by the demands of his new role. Seeking advice from friends and others who had worked with this new manager in the past might also have been helpful.

It may seem to some that fewer incidents of overt discrimination and harassment occur today than they used to, but to others it may seem like nothing has changed. If you are facing a serious situation, you may need help to address it. Be clear on your objectives, talk to trusted and savvy advisors about the best way to proceed, and decide on your next steps.

Sometimes bias exists on a systemic level. It exists in the processes and procedures of an organization. This is yet another reason for finding an organization that aligns with your values and has a culture in which you can thrive. If you find yourself in an organization with systemic bias, you have options. First of all, follow the guidance in this book. In addition, you may choose to get involved in solving the problem. Consider whether there is a way for this involvement to be a career-enhancing opportunity for you—refer to Chapter 10 for more information on this. If you decide that this challenge is insurmountable, then refer to Chapter 11 to help you think about whether, when, and how to move on.

Difficulty Establishing Relationships

People tend to like people like themselves, they tend to like to work with people like themselves, and they tend to like to promote people like themselves. When this natural affinity does not exist, it is often harder to establish significant mentor and sponsor relationships. It is harder to become part of the critical information networks that exist in organizations, and it is harder to be included in social activities where crucial business-related conversations happen.

Here are some strategies to address the challenges involved in building relationships with people who are not like you:

- **Be strategic and proactive.** If you are a member of an underrepresented group, it is essential that you are developing relationships strategically and proactively. Consider it a part of your job, and allocate time to it. Find ways to interact with people you want to develop relationships with. Make a practice of setting aside time for building relationships. Schedule phone calls, meetings, coffees, or lunches. If you're in an office, walk around and talk to people. Go back to the Relationship Network Assessment you completed in Chapter 6 and reexamine it. Identify any areas where you have faced challenges in building relationships, and think strategically about what you can do to build them.
- **Capitalize on spontaneous opportunities.** Take advantage of any impromptu opportunities that may arise to have a quality conversation. If you meet someone getting coffee or in the elevator, have a quick meaningful conversation and share enough about yourself and what you're doing to make them want to learn more. Consider following up and finding time for a longer conversation.
- **Highlight commonalities.** You may look different or come from different cultural backgrounds, and at the same time you may have

many things in common. Among them may be shared values, family circumstances, food preferences, experiences, or perspectives. I have worked with people who tell me that their colleagues are only interested in sports, and they have no interest in or knowledge of sports. If the people you work with have interests that you know nothing about, learn about those interests. Read and ask questions. You may gain a new interest, and if you don't, you will at least be able to participate in the conversation. Also, consider sharing your interests with others as a way to deepen your relationships.

- **Start building relationships from day one.** Don't wait until you have a crisis or challenge to start building relationships. Start building relationships now. Whenever you join a new department or organization, or begin working with new people, make building relationships a priority. If and when you have a challenge, you will have quality relationships in place that can help you.

- **Continually nurture and refresh your relationships.** Organizations change. They restructure. Leadership changes. People leave, and new people are hired. These changes can be challenging for members of underrepresented groups, as they must continually prove themselves to new people. Tend to your relationships and keep your relationship network fresh.

While it may be harder for you than for some others to develop quality relationships, it is definitely worth any added effort. The benefits of having quality relationships include better access to information, support, development, and career-enhancing opportunities. At the same time, the detrimental impact of *not* having relationships is real and can be harder to see, as in the example below.

Carlos: Carlos was an ambitious second-year associate at a large law firm. He wanted to someday be a partner at the firm, and decided that he would work harder than everyone else. At their official orientation,

Carlos and the other new associates were told that they would receive their assignments from the staffing coordinator. Carlos dutifully talked to the staffing coordinator to get his assignments. He had no idea that the best assignments were being given out by the partners themselves. Working on the right assignments with the right partners was the key to learning and developing quickly, gaining a reputation for being a star associate, and developing mentors and sponsors. While this was widely known, no one had told Carlos. Carlos was not part of the conversations where information like this was shared.

Carlos believed that all he had to do to succeed was to work hard. He did not understand the importance of relationships to his career, and he did not understand that he had to work harder than many others to build these relationships. If he had, Carlos could have begun building relationships from day one. He could have reached out to more people and deepened the level of conversation he had with other associates and partners. He could have accepted more invitations for social events and joined other lawyers when they were going to lunch or having a drink after work. Indeed, Carlos could have done everything I described in Chapter 6.

It is essential for you to be proactive and build relationships. Be strategic, and capitalize on opportunities to interact with people on a personal basis.

Being Overlooked for Opportunities

Given the existence of prejudice and the added difficulty of building relationships across perceived differences, it is not surprising to find that organizations often have trouble assessing and recognizing the potential of members of underrepresented groups. It is almost like they are invisible when high-potential talent is being discussed, and because of this they can be overlooked for opportunities. When selection committees are not diverse, it further decreases the chances that a diverse person will be selected for high-potential programs or a stretch assignment. To be invisible in an organization despite high performance is to be denied opportunities to excel and progress.

Here are some strategies to address this challenge:

- **Build relationships and raise your visibility with key decision makers.** Identify the key decision makers impacting your career. Find and create opportunities to interact meaningfully with them. Help them understand the value you bring to the organization.
- **Build relationships and raise your visibility with influencers.** Leaders often rely on a cadre of people to keep them informed about the talent within their areas. These influencers may include people who report to them, Human Resources professionals, and others who they know and respect. Build relationships with these influencers, and communicate your personal brand to them.
- **Let key decision makers and influencers know your aspirations and consider asking for their advice.** Let them know what you've achieved, what you are capable of, and what you want to do. Consider asking them for advice on how to take the next step in your career. There is a saying: "If you want help, ask for advice; and if you want advice, ask for help." If you don't have a strong relationship with someone already, you are likely to meet with more success if you ask for their advice rather than their help. If they are so inclined, they just may end up helping you.

Graham provides an example of how this dynamic can play out:

Graham: When a key leadership position opened up in his organization, Graham—a high-performing and highly respected African American man—stepped forward and expressed interest in the position. He was met with surprise. Somehow his name had not been on the initial list of candidates, although many of his white colleagues were being considered. Graham was certainly qualified and respected enough to have been on the initial list, but was somehow overlooked. In the end, Graham ended up being one of two finalists for the position. Graham's competence, credibility, and confidence were unquestioned, and Graham had developed quality relationships and had many supporters in the organization. Despite all this, he had still not been on the initial list of candidates.

Is there anything Graham could have done to have been included on the initial list of candidates? Graham already had the competence, credibility, relationships, and confidence to be effective and well respected. What he might have done was to let key decision makers know that he was interested in taking on more leadership within the organization, and that he aspired to the position in question. Nevertheless, while he was initially overlooked for the position, Graham did a great job of stepping forward and engaging in the process.

If you are a woman, person of color, or someone who is different from the leadership in your organization, you may face some of these additional challenges. Be strategic in addressing these challenges. Select work and an organization that aligns with your values, strengths, and interests, and develop your competence, credibility, confidence, and relationships. If, despite all of your efforts, you decide that you cannot make progress in your current organization, then your decision becomes whether, when, and how to move on. Chapter 11 discusses this decision in more detail.

Summary of Key Points

- If you feel like you don't fit in with your organizational culture or leadership and you are part of a group that is underrepresented in your organization, then you may be faced with some additional challenges. This may apply to women and people of color, as well as to those who feel different because of their sexual orientation, educational or socio-economic background, or a number of other dimensions.

- These unique organizational challenges fall into three general areas—facing stereotypes and bias, difficulty establishing relationships, and being overlooked for opportunities.

- Because of these challenges, it is critical to select work and an organization that align with your values, strengths, and interests, and to strategically and proactively develop your competence, credibility, confidence, and relationships.

- If you are facing an interaction where you suspect prejudice and bias is at play, analyze the situation and seek help from others. Adopt an attitude that allows you to deal constructively with the other person, and decide how best to proceed.

- To build strong relationships across differences, be strategic and proactive. Start building relationships from day one and make an effort to find and highlight commonalities with other people.

- To be more visible and recognized in your organization, build relationships and raise your visibility with key decision makers and their influencers. Share your aspirations with them and consider asking for their advice.

- If, despite all of your efforts, you decide that you cannot make progress in your current organization, then your decision becomes whether, when, and how to move on. Chapter 11 discusses this decision in more detail.

Personal Takeaways

Record your insights and respond to the questions on the following page.

What organizational challenges are you facing?

What will you do to address and overcome them?

Whose help do you need?

Chapter 9

LIMITING BELIEFS:
CHALLENGES FROM WITHIN

As you were reading Chapters 4–8, did you ever think to yourself "I can't do that," "That's not me," "I'm not good at that," or "I would never do that?" Underlying each of these thoughts is a belief that holds you back from engaging in behaviors or actions that are important to your career development. Some of these beliefs may be factual; others are actually fiction. These fictitious beliefs are called limiting beliefs, and it is critical to unmask these limiting beliefs so that they do not hold you back from realizing your career potential.

The only way to determine whether your beliefs are *fact* or *fiction* is to consciously identify and analyze them. If, after doing this, you determine that they are fiction and therefore limiting beliefs, then there are things you can do to replace them with more empowering beliefs. If, on the other hand, you determine that they are fact, then it is essential to review the relevant chapters in this book to determine your best course of action.

In my coaching, I've generally seen limiting beliefs emerge in four ways—from cultural values passed down through families and communities, from a desire to protect oneself, from imagined external barriers, or from an outdated or inaccurate sense of self. This chapter addresses these four types of limiting beliefs. If your limiting belief feels like a lack of confidence rather than one of the above, review Chapter 7.

The process of addressing limiting beliefs is a deeply personal one. I have included some tips below to help you with this process. Sometimes, all a person needs to successfully address these challenges is greater self-awareness. At other times, people need the help of a coach or counselor. If you fall into the latter category, I encourage you to enlist the help you need.

Cultural Values

Your cultural values reflect the family and community you grew up in, and include standards for what is appropriate and inappropriate behavior. If you work in an organizational culture that aligns with your cultural values, then you are most likely acting in congruence with its norms. If, however, you are working in an organization which is rooted in a different culture with different norms, then you may inadvertently act in a way that doesn't serve your career. Your cultural values may lead to limiting beliefs that hold you back from engaging in behaviors which are necessary for career advancement.

I am not suggesting that you change or discard your cultural values. Your cultural values are an important part of who you are. What I advocate is that you recognize and understand how your cultural values play out in your instinctive behaviors in the workplace. Once you have this awareness, then you have the power to develop the skills and choose the behaviors that will allow you to be most effective in your organization.

For example, if you grew up in a culture where you were taught to respect authority, a limiting belief might be that speaking up or challenging senior people is disrespectful and therefore something you do not do. This can be a problem in an organization where speaking up and challenging senior people is not only expected but valued. If you can identify this as a limiting belief, you can replace it with an empowering belief, such as: "The most respectful thing I can do to help senior people is to speak up and challenge them, so that they have the most accurate information possible and can make the best decisions." You can then build on this new empowering belief, and develop the skills to speak up in a respectful manner.

If you grew up in a culture where bragging was frowned upon, you may have developed the limiting belief that talking about your achievements is bragging and therefore something you don't do. This can be damaging in organizations where self-promotion is the norm. Alan provides an example of how cultural values can translate into instinctive behaviors and how, with awareness, you can develop the skills necessary to be more effective in the workplace.

Alan: Alan, an Asian American man, had always been careful about how he presented himself as he never wanted to be seen as bragging. Bragging was frowned upon in his family, and he neither did it nor respected others who did. When he was up for a big promotion, his manager reviewed the self-assessment he had written and asked him to rewrite it. She told him that it was "too humble" and did not reflect how much he had accomplished. Given that he wanted the promotion, he decided to ask a colleague if he could read his self-assessment for ideas. When Alan read his colleague's self-assessment, he was surprised at how often his colleague used "I" instead of "we." He noticed that his colleague used different words to describe his actions—words like "lead," "responsible for," "initiated," and "achieved." This was in sharp contrast to the words Alan used, such as "participated in," "carried out," and "completed." His colleague also used adjectives like "outstanding" and "exceptional"—words Alan had never used to describe himself or his work. After reading his colleague's self-assessment and realizing that this was what senior people were used to seeing, he rewrote his own self-assessment. He was still uncomfortable, but at the same time he realized that it was a more accurate representation of what he had done.

Alan realized that his cultural value of not bragging had led him to instinctively underrepresent his own accomplishments. With his new-found awareness, he decided to adopt the empowering belief that he could remain true to himself and help his career by simply sharing facts about what he had done and describing his accomplishments more accurately. He considered this a skill that he could develop.

Your cultural values may lie at the core of some of your limiting beliefs. Here are some tips for identifying and addressing limiting beliefs arising out of differences between your cultural values and your organization's values:

- Become more aware of your cultural values and the way they impact your behavior. Consider your approach to communication, conflict, and relationships. Consider your approach to time, decision-making, and hierarchy.
- Identify the circumstances in which your cultural values are in line with your organization's culture, and those in which they run counter to the norms of your organization.
- Identify your limiting beliefs and find ways to turn them into empowering beliefs. For example, instead of thinking "I don't talk about my accomplishments because that's bragging," try thinking "I share the facts about my achievements without embellishment or exaggeration."
- Learn and develop new approaches, strategies, and skills so that you can be as effective as possible in your organization. Ask for help from your manager, peers, and mentors. Practice these new skills and ask for feedback.
- Stay authentic, and at the same time, allow yourself to develop and grow.
- Look for opportunities to share your culture with others in your organization. This will help them better understand your cultural values.

Self-Protection

People often develop limiting beliefs as a self-protective mechanism. They may have had a negative experience in the past, or they may be afraid of something that might happen in the future. Some of the most common fears that hold people back are fear of rejection, failure, and embarrassment.

Jan provides an example of a limiting belief arising from a desire to not repeat a past negative experience.

> **Jan:** Despite having many new ideas, Jan felt that she could not speak up and share them with her boss. After all, she had done this once before and gotten burned. She had come up with an idea for how the department could implement a process improvement, developed the idea, and presented it to her boss. She then watched as her boss handed the opportunity to someone else in her department without giving her any credit or role in the implementation. After this experience, and even though she continued to have great ideas, Jan stayed silent and did not speak up. She was afraid that she would be burned again. She thought she was protecting herself, but ultimately realized that she was hurting her own career by not speaking up. With the help of a coach, she strategized on how to present her next idea, and decided to do it in an open forum with many people present. She also worked on developing more relationships and made it a point to talk to many people about her ideas before sharing them at meetings.

It wasn't easy for Jan to reengage, but she decided that she needed to find a way to express her ideas and get credit for them to progress in her career.

Here are some tips for addressing limiting beliefs and behaviors arising from a desire for self-protection:

- If you find yourself holding back from doing something that might help your career, ask yourself if your hesitancy is arising from fear and a desire to protect yourself in some way. It may be that your instinct is right, and that this is a behavior you should not be engaging in. Or, it may be that this behavior would be beneficial to your career, and you should find the courage to proceed. Ask yourself whether the circumstances are different now than before, or whether you are better equipped now than before, or whether there are things you can do now to mitigate the risk.
- Ask trusted mentors or colleagues for advice. Describe the situation and ask them to help you decide upon the best course of action.
- Change the limiting belief "I can't do X" to an empowering belief. You might restate it as "I can do X, if I do Y first." Or "I couldn't do X before, but now I can."
- Develop the skills and resources necessary to be successful in this situation.
- Once you engage in the behavior, ask for feedback from trusted colleagues. Assess what you did well and how you can improve.

Imagined External Barriers

Sometimes we believe that we are being held back by some external circumstance, when the truth is that we are holding ourselves back. This limiting belief often feels like a fact unless carefully examined. I have worked with women who feel that they can't achieve their career goals because they have children. For some of them, this may be true. For others, it is a fiction. With coaching, I have seen some women come up with real solutions. I've heard women say, "My husband can stay with the kids one night a week," or "Actually, my mother has been asking for more time with the kids. She could babysit and they would love it," or "I can ask to work at home one day a week, and that would allow me to stay later on other days."

One way to identify whether you are dealing with a real or imagined external barrier is to restate your belief statement as an assumption statement. For example, instead of saying "I can't do X because of Y," you could say, "I have been assuming that I can't do X because of Y." Now, there's an opening to ask, "What if I could? What would I do?" Here's an example of how this approach works:

> **Phillip:** Phillip was assigned to what he considered a dead-end project. He wanted to stay at his organization and transfer off the project, but he believed that transferring was impossible. After all, there were other people on the project team who had been there longer than him who wanted to transfer off, and he felt like he was an indispensable part of the team. With the help of a coach, Phillip realized that he could transfer if he made a strong business case and groomed his successor. He identified a younger person on the team who had the potential to take over if he spent a little more time developing her. Phillip also put together a well-thought-out business case for him to transfer to another project, and began speaking to and lining up support from a few senior people. It took about six months, but ultimately Phillip transferred to a much more desirable assignment.

Initially, Phillip believed that transferring was impossible. It was only after realizing that he had created an imaginary external barrier that Phillip was able to create options for himself and ultimately transfer.

Here are some tips for addressing imagined external barriers:

- Explore whether you're dealing with a real or imagined external barrier. If there is something you feel like you can't do, take a moment and reframe your belief statement. Replace the clause "I believe I can't..." with "I have been assuming that I can't..." If reframing starts opening up some hope or possibilities, that's an indication that you may have identified an imagined external barrier.
- Once you reframe your statement, ask yourself, "What's possible? How can I achieve my objectives?" Then develop a plan of action.

- It may be helpful to talk to a mentor, coach, or counselor. There may be a deep-seated reason you've been thinking the way you do, and addressing the underlying reason may be important.

Outdated or Inaccurate Sense of Self

Sometimes limiting beliefs come from a sense of self that is outdated or inaccurate. I've heard people say things like "I'm not good with people," "I'm horrible at making presentations," or "I'm terrible at networking." And when they examine these beliefs more deeply, they discover that, while this may have been true in the past, it no longer applies because they have developed and grown since then. The belief is outdated and inaccurate—it is fiction and not fact.

I've noticed that some people who are making the transition from individual contributor to leader continue to see themselves as a person who is great at getting the work done. Their sense of self hasn't caught up with who they have become, and until it does, it is difficult for them to act like a leader. Leonard is an example of this dynamic.

Leonard: Leonard was a top performer in a consulting firm. He did exemplary work, had a "do whatever it takes" attitude, and was relied on heavily by senior people. As he approached the point of being considered for partner, he began to hear feedback that he "didn't command the room," "needed to be more strategic," and "lacked executive presence"—all of which were critical for a partner. Leonard started working with a coach and realized that he thought of himself as someone who was great at doing the work. He did not think of himself as a partner. With the help of his coach, he visualized what it would look like and feel like to be a partner. Before walking into a meeting, he intentionally put on his partner mindset, and then acted as if he was a partner. Once he did this, there was noticeable improvement in his executive presence and ability to command the room. Adopting this mindset made it easier for Leonard to develop the skills he needed, and helped him ultimately become a partner.

Here are some tips for dealing with limiting beliefs that arise from an outdated or inaccurate sense of self.

- Think about how you view yourself. Do you see yourself as someone who fits your past role, your current role, or your desired future role?
- If you see yourself most comfortably in your past role, think about who you are now and what you need to do to shift your mindset to identify with your current role. If your eyes are on your next role, think about what you need to do to shift your mindset to identify with that role.
- If your sense of self is outdated, I encourage you to reframe your thinking. Instead of thinking "I'm not good at X," try "I wasn't good at X in the past, but I am now," or "I wasn't good at X in the past, but I'm getting better." Don't let limiting beliefs hold you back from developing the skills you need now.
- If you want to shift your mindset, try a visualization exercise. Imagine yourself truly being comfortable in your role. Imagine how you would feel and act and think. Imagine how you would enter a room and carry yourself—where you would sit, how you would speak, what kinds of things you would say. Come up with a mantra, an image, or a name for this persona. Call upon it when you want to move into this mindset, and then act accordingly.

Addressing Limiting Beliefs

When limiting beliefs arise, they feel real. If you notice yourself holding back or believing that you cannot take action as described in this book, ask yourself what your underlying beliefs are. Consciously identify and analyze your underlying beliefs to determine whether they are *fact* or *fiction*. If you determine that they are fiction, replace them with empowering beliefs and build the skills you need to move ahead in your career.

Summary of Key Points

- As you were reading Chapters 4–8, did you ever think to yourself "I can't do that," "That's not me," "I'm not good at that," or "I would never do that"? Underlying these thoughts is a belief that is holding you back from engaging in behaviors or actions which are important to your career development.
- Some of these beliefs may be factual; others are actually fiction. These fictitious beliefs are called limiting beliefs, and it is critical to unmask these limiting beliefs so that they do not hold you back in your career.
- The only way to determine whether your beliefs are *fact* or *fiction* is to consciously identify and analyze them. If you determine that they are fiction, then there are things you can do to replace them with more empowering beliefs. If they are fact, then it is essential to review the relevant chapters of this book and determine your best course of action.
- Limiting beliefs can emerge from cultural values passed down through families and communities. They can emerge from a desire to protect yourself, from imagined external barriers, or from an outdated or inaccurate sense of self. There are techniques you can use in each of these cases to turn limiting beliefs into empowering beliefs.
- The process of addressing limiting beliefs is a deeply personal one. Sometimes, all a person needs to successfully address these challenges is greater self-awareness. At other times, people need the help of a coach or counselor. If you fall in this latter category, I encourage you to enlist the help you need.

Personal Takeaways

Record your insights and respond to the questions on the following page.

What limiting beliefs do you have, and how are they holding you back from engaging in behaviors that are important to your career development?

What can you do to address your limiting beliefs and replace them with empowering beliefs?

Whose help do you need?

OPPORTUNITY

PREPARATION

FOUNDATION

Part III:
OPPORTUNITY

Chapter 10

-- ↗

RECOGNIZING AND CREATING OPPORTUNITY

Luck happens when preparation meets opportunity. Your career opportunities may come in many forms—a conversation, chance encounter, assignment, request, or project. When you are prepared for and alert to opportunities, you are more likely to recognize and create them.

Here are some examples of opportunities that were recognized or created:

> **Beverly:** "I've been invited to participate in my company's high-potential leadership program. It's intense—there are four off-site sessions and a yearlong project you work on and present to the Executive Committee. I'm really busy with work, and I have a family. It's a huge additional time commitment, and I am going to do it. It's an incredible opportunity to develop my leadership skills, gain visibility with the Executive Committee, expand my network across the company, and learn about the strategic issues the company is facing. It's also a nomination program—the senior people in my division picked me out of all my peers for this program. That shows they have a lot of confidence in me and want to invest in me. This is an opportunity I can't pass up."

Peter: "My manager approached me one day with what he called an 'opportunity' with air quotes. It was one of those thankless tasks with no upside. If you did it well, no one would notice; but if you did it poorly, everyone would know. I thought hard about how I could make this into an actual opportunity with an upside, and decided that I would not just complete the task, but would streamline and improve the process at the same time. I did it, and my manager was really appreciative. I ended up getting a lot of recognition from some very senior people."

Donna: "I was in a dead-end job. I wanted to stay at my company and do something else, but I didn't know what I wanted to do. I started going to events where I could meet people from other departments. When I met new people, I tried to get to know them and asked them about the kind of work they did. I met Joyce at a volunteer event and told her that I wanted to make a move. Joyce told me about an open position in her department, and offered to introduce me to her manager. They ended up hiring me, even though I had no experience in the area."

Sangcheon: "I've been telling people ever since I joined the firm that I speak Korean and wanted an overseas assignment in Korea. It's taken a few years, but I was just asked to go to Korea for two months on a short-term assignment. They needed someone with Korean language skills on the team, and they remembered what I had said."

Felix: "A year ago, I was running a department in our technology operation. The technology functions were pretty siloed, and we were having difficulty working with another department on a project that required a lot of collaboration. I could see from a business perspective that it made sense for these two functions to be under one umbrella, so I developed and presented a business case to the head of the division to consolidate the two areas under my leadership. She agreed. I went from having 150 people in my department to 500 people. We decreased the time it took to complete our projects and improved the quality of our deliverables at the same time."

Let's take a closer look at these stories. Beverly and Peter are examples of people who *recognized* opportunity when it came knocking. Beverly was handed a gift-wrapped opportunity in the form of a high-potential program, while Peter was handed an opportunity masquerading as a thankless task.

Donna and Sangcheon proactively *created* their opportunities. Donna made it a point to meet people in other departments and have conversations that might lead to job opportunities. Sangcheon let others know about his language skills and desire for an overseas assignment so as to be top of mind when that need arose.

Felix *recognized and created* his next opportunity. He identified an unrecognized business need and then created his opportunity by developing and presenting the business case for combining the two functions under his leadership.

Recognizing Opportunities

Sometimes opportunity comes in a neat, gift-wrapped package, as in the example of Beverly above. Sometimes it masquerades as a thankless or messy assignment that no one wants, as in the example of Peter above. You may hear a manager or sponsor say, "This is your ticket to the next level. Do a great job, and you will have a lot of support for promotion." Or, you may hear, "No one wants to do this. This is an impossible assignment." In either case, your first step is to assess the situation and determine whether this is a career-enhancing opportunity and whether you can succeed at it. Seek the advice of your mentors and ask yourself the following:

- What is the opportunity exactly, and how will success be measured?
- What additional information do I need about the opportunity?
- What is the best possible outcome for me if I take this on?
- What do I need to do to achieve this best possible outcome?
- Do I have the skills to succeed? If not, how can I develop the skills or form a team with the necessary skills?
- What resources do I need to succeed, and how can I get these resources?
- How much time do I realistically need to achieve results?
- Whose help and support do I need?
- What is the most likely outcome?
- What is the potential downside of accepting this opportunity?
- How can I mitigate or manage the downside?
- If I accept this opportunity, what does it mean for my other work?
- What are the potential consequences of not accepting this opportunity?

This is where your preparation will make a difference. If you've been working on your competence, credibility, relationships, and confidence, your chances of succeeding and exceeding expectations will be much higher.

Creating Opportunities

Creating career-building opportunities requires being proactive. For Donna in the example above, it meant finding ways to meet people. For Sangcheon, it meant speaking up and letting others know about his skills. And for Felix, it meant writing and presenting a proposal to address a business need. In every case, these career-building opportunities met an organizational need.

As you think about creating your own opportunities, ask yourself:

- What opportunities can I identify or create for my organization? How can I help my organization capitalize on them?
- What are some of the unrecognized or unmet needs of my organization? How can I help meet these needs?
- How can processes or products be improved? What can I do to help make these improvements?
- Who are the key people in my organization? How can I help make their jobs easier?
- What are my unique skills or talents that have value for the organization? How can I use them to help my organization?

Notice that each of the above questions has two parts. The first is asking about an area of opportunity for your organization. The second is asking about what you can do to help your organization capitalize on this opportunity. After you uncover potential opportunities for yourself, go back to the previous section and review the questions under Recognizing Opportunities. Then decide upon your next course of action.

Here's an example of creating an opportunity:

Kiara: Kiara managed to create an opportunity during an interview with a potential employer. As she was discussing the position with the hiring manager, she asked a lot of questions, listened carefully, and came to the realization that the position needed to be modified if it was going to fill the need the organization was looking to address. She shared her thoughts with the interviewer, and described how she was uniquely suited to fill that position. She ended up getting hired to fill the position she essentially created.

Lost Opportunities

Opportunities can be hard to spot in the moment, unless you are looking for them. Here are two examples of opportunities that were lost because they weren't recognized:

Lisa: "Several years ago, I was leading a brand-new initiative that required working with many people within the organization. It was such a great opportunity to build my career, and I completely mismanaged it. I was so focused on getting the work done that I wasn't strategic in *how* I got it done. The biggest missed opportunity happened when I asked another person who was almost at my level to work with a particular senior executive. I could have worked with the executive myself, but I didn't recognize it as an opportunity to build a key relationship and increase my credibility. Well, the guy who worked with the senior executive ended up getting promoted, and I never did get the credit for all my hard work. If I had to do it over again, I would have done the same great work and also used every interaction with a senior person as an opportunity to build a relationship."

Chris: "I was complaining that there weren't enough African Americans in leadership at my company, and my coach asked me why I hadn't taken on more leadership—after all, I was one of the most experienced African Americans in the company. As we talked, I remembered that I had been asked to take on more senior leadership roles several times in the past. Each time, I had turned it down because I was so focused on my own work. I guess those were actually my opportunities to become a leader in this company."

Think about your own lost opportunities. Perhaps you did not take advantage of an opportunity to meet someone, to learn something new, or to communicate a skill or accomplishment. Perhaps you shied away from an opportunity to make a presentation, to take a leadership role, or to share an idea or opinion in a meeting. Learn from these experiences. Ask yourself whether you would do things differently if you had known then what you know now and been actively managing your career.

To increase your chances of recognizing opportunities in the moment, adopt the mindset that there are many opportunities around you. By assuming that you have opportunities, you will see more opportunities. Now, with that mindset, which of your many opportunities will you seize?

Career Luck: Preparation Meeting Opportunity

This book has been full of examples of preparation meeting opportunity. Let's reexamine the stories of a few of the people you met in earlier chapters. The parts of their stories in which they recognized and created their opportunities are italicized.

Ana from Chapter 2: After high school, Ana got a job as a receptionist at a manufacturing company. She was bored, and curious about other jobs at the company. *Ana loved a challenge, and when she overheard a friend in the controller's office talk about how no one could figure something out, she asked if she could try it. She had always been good with numbers. To her amazement, her friend said yes and explained what they were trying to do. Ana worked all weekend, figured it out, and brought the completed work back to her friend.* She was soon recruited into a position in the controller's office. Ana earned her college degree and eventually worked her way up to becoming a controller. She found the industry fascinating and never grew tired of the challenge of accounting. Ana loved her job and thrived in her career.

Teresa from Chapter 3: In college, Teresa's favorite classes were in finance and game theory. She interned at an investment bank and, while she thought the work was interesting, she did not appreciate the brutal hours. After graduating, she joined a private equity firm where, as she put it, "I can do interesting work and I don't have to work every weekend." She spent four years at the private equity firm and decided that, in addition to interesting work and more civilized hours, she also wanted to work in an environment that was more supportive, with a manager who cared about her development, and where she could really grow professionally. *She spent six months searching for the right position, and she ended up working at a hedge fund that met all her requirements.*

Andres from Chapter 4: Andres was a young associate in corporate finance at an investment bank. *He was so interested in learning about companies and their businesses that, in his free time, he studied offering prospectuses. He brought his deep understanding of industries and companies to his work in corporate finance, and stood out as someone with extraordinary expertise in analyzing businesses.* His firm ultimately asked him to transfer to a new high-growth area where he could use this knowledge more directly.

Justin from Chapter 5: *Justin, a single father, noticed that while his company had groups and events for working mothers, it did not have similar groups or events for working fathers. After speaking to a few senior men who were enthusiastic about the idea, Justin started the first-ever fathers group at his organization. He led the first meeting,* *which was well attended, and was recognized for his effort by several senior executives.*

Charles from Chapter 6: Charles liked people, enjoyed interacting with them, and derived a lot of energy from these interactions. *When he went to the coffee station on his floor, he greeted whoever was there. Sometimes, both he and the other person were looking for a break, and so what could have been a brief greeting became a longer conversation. When a new person joined the department, he introduced himself, tried to learn more about them, and offered to help them out. He enjoyed going to company events where he was able to see friends and meet interesting new people. Everyone worked hard at his company, so Charles was always respectful of other people's time. Charles was also aware of who the senior people were in his company. He made a special effort to talk with them whenever he had the opportunity. At events, before approaching someone he hadn't met before, he would quickly think about how he would introduce himself, what questions he might ask, and what information he wanted to share.*

Katherine from Chapter 7: Katherine is one of the leaders of her Employee Resource Group. *She had the idea of creating her company's first-ever ERG Professional Development Conference. She asked the leaders of the other ERGs in her company whether their groups would like to co-sponsor the event. She invited executives to attend and speak, and on the day of the event she stepped to the podium in the role of Master of Ceremonies.* She had never done anything of this magnitude before, but she had experienced a lot of success in her role at the company, and she knew she could do it. Her confidence and enthusiasm energized the group and led to a highly successful event.

Luck happens when preparation meets opportunity. In Chapters 1–3, you set your foundation. In Chapters 4–9, you prepared. And in this chapter, you explored how to recognize and create opportunities. The next chapter addresses how to decide whether, when, and how to move on from your current position.

Summary of Key Points

- Luck happens when preparation meets opportunity.
- Your career opportunities may come in many forms—a conversation, encounter, relationship, assignment, or project.
- Sometimes opportunity presents itself in a neat, gift-wrapped package. Sometimes it masquerades as a messy assignment that no one wants. In either case, your first step is to assess the situation and determine whether this truly is a career-enhancing opportunity you want to accept.
- Creating opportunities requires being proactive. Look for ways to meet an organizational need and create value for your organization.
- To increase your chances of recognizing opportunities in the moment, adopt the mindset that you have many opportunities around you.

Personal Takeaways

Record your insights and respond to the question on the following page.

List 10 opportunities you have now.

List 10 opportunities you can create.

What opportunities will you accept or create?

Chapter 11

MOVING ON

Long gone are the days when someone joined a company out of college and worked there for the rest of their lives. Today, changing jobs and companies is almost expected. The challenge is to make every career move an intentional, thoughtful, and meaningful one.

The Physics of Changing Jobs: Push and Pull

I have noticed that there are two forces at work when someone decides to change jobs—a push and a pull. The push is the motivation to *move away* from something and the pull is the motivation to *move toward* something else. The intensity of the push depends on the pain and discomfort felt in their current position. The intensity of the pull depends on how attractive and desirable another position is.

When there is little to no push and someone is feeling no pain in their current position, they need a truly compelling opportunity to decide to leave. When there is a strong push and someone is feeling a high degree of pain, they will leave based on nothing more than the hope of something better.

These next two stories illustrate this dynamic:

Jill: "I was very happy in my position—I liked my work and my boss, and I had a lot of opportunities. Then my boss left, and I could not stand the new person who came in. She changed what we did and how we operated, and she took me away from the work I loved. One day a friend of mine called, and when she asked me how I was, I blurted out, 'I hate it here.' Her response was, 'We're looking for another person. How about joining us?' I scheduled an interview with her boss, and two weeks later I walked into a new job. It turned out not to be the right job for me, but at that moment I didn't care. I just wanted to leave."

Lucas: "I started an internet company with some friends a few years back when we were in grad school. After we graduated, the other two devoted themselves full-time to the company while I followed my parents' advice and took a 'safe' job in finance. I kept my equity and stayed involved on the side. I was very happy in my finance position. Then, our internet company started doing really well. It was growing fast, and my friends asked me to come back as CFO. When I told people about the opportunity, they thought I was nuts not to grab it, but I was happy where I was, so it took me a few weeks to decide. Ultimately, I took the job—it was just too good to pass up."

In the first example, Jill hated her new boss and was feeling a push so strong that she jumped at the first opportunity that presented itself, even though it might not have been the best fit for her. Lucas, on the other hand, enjoyed his job and was feeling no pain. It took a truly compelling opportunity to get him to move.

Analyzing Your Push and Pull Factors

When someone is feeling a strong push or pull, there are often intense emotions accompanying it. A strong push is often accompanied by feelings of pain, frustration, disappointment, anger, or even hate. A strong pull is often accompanied by feelings of euphoria, excitement, desire, or love. It is helpful to examine and analyze your push and pull factors so that you can better understand your emotions and make the best decision for you and your career.

There are many factors that can lead to someone feeling a push. Here are some of the most common push factors I've heard about:

- You feel like you can't progress in this organization
- You feel like you can't grow or learn new things in your current position
- You have serious difficulty with your manager or some other influential person
- You're feeling insecure in your position
- You're fearful about an impending reorganization
- You're negatively impacted by a reorganization or leadership change
- You don't enjoy your work and don't look forward to going to work
- Your personal circumstances have changed and your job is no longer a good fit

Push factors can be temporary or permanent. They may arise from an organizational challenge, as described in Chapter 8, or from a limiting belief, as described in Chapter 9. You may be able to minimize or alleviate the push factor by taking some action. The intensity of the push you feel may waver, diminish, or grow over time.

The following exercise will help you examine and explore your emotions and any push and pull factors you may be experiencing now. Find a quiet moment without distractions, and give yourself time to think through the following questions. Be as specific as you can. Notice how much emotion this exercise engenders for you.

EXERCISE: ASSESSING YOUR PUSH AND PULL FACTORS

PART I. Push Factors

Describe the quality and strength of the emotion you feel when thinking about your current position.

What specifically is it about your current position that you want to leave behind?

Is there an organizational challenge or a limiting belief behind your desire to leave? If so, what is it specifically, and what can you do to address it?

Is this a temporary or permanent circumstance?

What can you do to lessen or alleviate the pain you feel in your current position?

Do you want to leave your company, or do you want to stay at your company and leave your position?

On a scale of 0 to 5, how would you rate the strength of the push you are feeling? 0 means "nonexistent" and 5 means "overwhelming."

PART 2. Pull Factors

Describe the position or type of position you are considering moving into.

Describe the quality and strength of the emotion you feel when thinking about your desired position.

What specifically is it about this new position that is attractive to you?

How does this position align with your values, strengths, and interests?

How does this position help you reach your long-term goals?

Do you have this opportunity in hand, or do you need to search for it?

On a scale of 0 to 5, how would you rate the strength of the pull you are feeling? 0 means "nonexistent" and 5 means "overwhelming."

Deciding Whether, When, and How to Move On

Now that you understand your push and pull factors, and the emotions involved on both ends, it's time to decide whether, when, and how to move on. The steps outlined below can help you make the best decision. You may not go through these steps in this order, but make sure you review and address each step before making your final decision.

Make sure you are in a positive emotional state before engaging in this process.

- If you're feeling a strong push and a high level of stress, take steps to get to a better emotional state before making any big decisions. Consider taking a vacation or giving yourself a chance to decompress before deciding on making a move. If you can find a way to decrease the stress you are feeling, you will be more able to make a well-informed and thoughtful decision about moving for the *right* opportunity as opposed to the *first* opportunity.

Go back to your foundation.

- Review your values, strengths, and interests. Go back to Chapter 2 and review the exercises. Your answers may have changed since the first time you completed these exercises. Understanding your values, strengths, and interests will help you make sense of your current situation and assess your fit with possible future positions.
- Review your goals. Go back to Chapter 3 and reassess your goals. Ask yourself whether your current position will help you reach your goals, or whether there is a better route to reaching your goals.

Analyze your current position.

- Ask yourself if you've made the most of your current position. Review Chapters 1 through 10. Ask yourself whether there is anything more you can do to develop in your current position.

What else can you learn? What additional skills can you develop? What other relationships can you foster? What opportunities can you create? How can you modify your position to better meet your needs? Make a list of the action steps you may be able to take now to improve your chances of becoming luckier in your current position.

- Consult your mentors and trusted colleagues. Use your judgment on when and how to talk to people you trust about your situation, and get their advice and counsel. Try to get different perspectives and learn from people with different experiences. Talk to people who will ask you tough questions and engage in difficult conversations to help you make the best decision. They may tell you something about your current situation that you aren't aware of. They may know of an opening or start listening for opportunities for you.

- Consider whether there is an optimal time to make a move. Your job search may be best served by having one more significant achievement or skill on your resume, or by timing your job search to match the hiring cycle in your industry. Consider your circumstances and think about the optimal time to move. Do what you can to make your remaining time in your current job productive and worthwhile.

Decide whether to stay in your current position or explore options for moving on.

- If you decide to stay in your current position, continue to follow the guidance in this book to maximize your experience. Reassess your decision periodically.
- If you decide to explore options for moving on,
  - ▶ Reassess and refresh your personal brand. Review Chapter 5 and update your personal brand. Prepare stories and anecdotes you can use to help communicate your brand.

▶ Look for and create options. Decide upon a search strategy. Activate your internal and external networks.

▶ If you're looking for job opportunities within your company, consider when and how to tell your current manager and others you work with. Take into consideration your organization's norms and practices for this process. Look at the relationship network you outlined in Chapter 6 and update it. Make a list of the people you want to talk to about a possible transfer. Don't wait for a job posting. Oftentimes, jobs are posted only after the department has identified the person they want to hire.

▶ If you decide that now is the time for you to go back to school and build up your credentials, be clear on what you want to gain from this experience. Some people want the degree behind their name, others want access to a new network of people, and still others want to transition into a new career altogether. Make sure the degree and school you select will lead to the outcome you want.

▶ If you decide that now is the time for you to start your own business, think about whether there is anything else you need to do before you leave to start your business. Consider whether there are additional skills you want to build, money you want to save, or people you want to meet before you leave your company. Consider whether you want your current company to be your first client.

▶ If you decide that you want to leave the workforce altogether, think about how long you plan on being away and what your long-term career goals are. Decide whether there is anything you want to do to stay informed about your industry, whether there are any licenses or credentials you want to keep current, and whether there are any professional relationships you want to maintain.

▸ Analyze options in light of your values, strengths, interests, and goals. You have the tools to assess your options. Ask yourself whether the opportunity is in alignment with your values, strengths, and interests, and whether it can help you achieve your long-term goals. Ask yourself whether the culture of the organization you are considering joining is one in which you can thrive.

▸ Do your due diligence. Once you've identified an opportunity, do your due diligence. Talk to people, ask questions, and do an internet search for information. Try to determine how closely your expectations will match the reality of the new position. If you're considering another job, find out more about the person you will be working for, and the people you will be working with. Try to ascertain whether your new manager has a history of developing and promoting people. Assess whether you will have the resources you need to succeed in this role.

Once you've identified an opportunity, decide whether to accept a new opportunity, continue exploring options, or stay in your current position.

- If you decide to accept a new opportunity, *leave in good graces*. Once you accept another position or decide to leave, think hard about what and how you'll tell your current organization. Don't burn bridges. You never know when you'll meet up with these people again. They could turn up as your client, peer, or manager in another organization, or as an informal reference. Refer back to the earlier chapters in this book and *prepare for your next position*. Remember to start building relationships from day one.

- If you decide to continue exploring, refer back to the process outlined above.

- If you decide to stay in your current position, continue to follow the guidance in this book to maximize your experience. Reassess your decision periodically.

One of the principles this book is based on is that you are a whole person and need to think about your career in the context of your whole life. Remember to consider the implications of a move on your personal life.

Summary of Key Points

- Make every career move an intentional, thoughtful, and meaningful one.
- There are two forces at work when someone decides to change jobs—a push and a pull. The push is the motivation to *move away* from something and is based on the pain and discomfort felt in someone's current position. The pull is the motivation to *move toward* something else and depends on how attractive and desirable the other position is.
- Make sure you are in a positive emotional state before making the decision.
- Go back to your foundation and review your values, strengths, interests, and goals.
- Analyze your current position and consult your mentors and trusted colleagues.
- Decide whether to stay in your current position or explore options for moving on.
- Analyze options in light of your values, strengths, interests, and goals. Do your due diligence.
- If you decide to move on, leave in good graces and prepare for your next position.
- Think about your move in the context of your whole life.

Personal Takeaways

Record your insights and answer the questions on the following page.

If you're considering a move:

What are your push and pull factors?

How can you move into a positive emotional state before making this important decision?

Who will you talk to about this decision?

What will your next steps be?

Chapter 12

CREATING YOUR CAREER GAME PLAN

*You leap out of bed on Monday morning, excited to start your day. You enjoy thinking about work, even on your days off. Your work is something you **want** to do, instead of something you **have** to do.*

This is the vision set out for you at the very beginning of this book. This is what can happen when your work is in alignment with your values, strengths, and interests. This is what can happen when you are fully prepared and maximize your opportunities. This is what can happen when you lead your way.

Summary of What's Been Covered

We've covered a lot of ground in this book. Here is a quick summary:

- Luck happens when preparation meets opportunity. To be luckier in your career, set a strong foundation, do the preparation, and recognize and create your opportunities.
- The more you align your career with your personal values, strengths, and interests, the more energy, engagement, and fulfillment you'll experience.
- Create destination or directional goals so that you can proactively and intentionally move in the direction you want to go.

- Having a consistently high level of competence and performance is a critical component of moving your career forward. Develop a deep level of expertise, continually master new technical and social skills, and understand and learn from your experiences and feedback.

- You are your own personal brand manager. Create, communicate, monitor, update, and enhance your personal brand in order to develop a reputation that reflects who you are at your best and helps you achieve your goals.

- Having strong and diverse relationships can power your career development by giving you access to information, mentorship, sponsorship, and much-needed support. Build relationships now and continually nurture, maintain, and expand your relationships throughout your career.

- Develop your confidence in yourself, your capabilities, and your ability to succeed. Having a high degree of confidence will help you engage in more challenging and visible activities, increase your resilience and ability to recover from negative experiences, and help you persevere in the face of challenging situations.

- Women, people of color, and others who are different from the leadership in their organizations may face unique organizational challenges in the form of stereotypes and bias, difficulty building relationships, and being overlooked for opportunities. Be aware of these challenges, and do what you can to minimize them preemptively. If you are facing them, be strategic and intentional in how you address them.

- Limiting beliefs come from within and, if not recognized and managed, can slow down or hinder your career. If you are subject to limiting beliefs, become more self-aware, identify your limiting beliefs, and transform them into empowering beliefs.

- You have many opportunities around you. Expect them, look for them, and create them. Assess each opportunity and decide whether this is an opportunity you are prepared for and one that can lead you on a path to realizing your career aspirations.

- Make every career move an intentional and meaningful one. Be thoughtful about whether, when, and how to move on.

Your Career Game Plan

You may have already taken significant steps to move your career forward, or you may be wondering how you are going to make all of this happen.

In the following exercise, you will create a Career Game Plan. There are three parts to this exercise. In the first part, you will record your touchstones for making decisions—namely your values, strengths, interests, and goals. In the second part, you will create monthly goals and schedule weekly activities to meet your monthly goals. The third part will give you a tool to monitor and measure your progress.

CAREER GAME PLAN

Date:

PART I. Foundation

List your values, strengths, and interests. These will serve as touch-stones for your career decisions.

Record your long-term and short-term goals. These will serve as reference points for your monthly goals.

Values	Strengths	Interests

Long-term goals

Short-term goals

PART 2. Action Plan

At the beginning of each month, set one-month goals designed to help you achieve your short-term and long-term goals.

Date:_____

This month's goals:

At the beginning of each week, decide upon and record the actions you will take to achieve your one-month goals. Schedule these activities on your calendar.

Week 1 Activities:

Week 2 Activities:

Week 3 Activities:

Week 4 Activities:

PART 3. Progress Report

The dashboard below will help you keep track of your progress. At the end of each month, answer "yes" or "no" to the questions and tally up the number of "yes" answers at the bottom. This form will take you through one full year.

Starting Date: _____

Months:

	1	2	3	4	5	6	7	8	9	10	11	12
1. Are you satisfied with your progress on your one-month goals?												
2. Are you satisfied with your progress on developing your competence?												
3. Are you satisfied with your progress on developing your credibility?												
4. Are you satisfied with your progress on developing your relationships?												
5. Are you satisfied with the level of confidence you're experiencing?												
6. Have you formulated your goals for the next month?												
Add up the number of "yes" responses:												

As your year progresses, notice if there are any trends, and ask yourself the following questions:

- To which questions do you consistently answer "yes"?
- To which questions do you consistently answer "no"?
- What are you doing well?
- What do you want to start doing?
- What do you want to stop doing?
- What do you want to continue to do?
- What are you learning?
- What's holding you back?
- Whose help do you need to move forward?

By actively measuring your progress, you can be intentional about your next steps. You may decide to adjust some of your goals, or you may decide to adjust some of your actions. Stay true to yourself and move in the direction you want to go.

Lead Your Way

This book is meant to be lived. Reading is just the start. The real learning and progress will happen when you move into action. You now know what to do to create the career you want. Take action. Reflect on your experience. Ask yourself what worked and what didn't, what you want to repeat and what you won't do again. Learn from your experiences, and apply that learning going forward.

Stay true to your personal values and to yourself. Your career journey will have twists and turns. Come back to this book periodically. Review these concepts as new situations arise. Touch base with your values, strengths, and interests. Update your goals and your Career Game Plan. Keep learning. Stay prepared and alert to opportunities. Be proactive and move in the direction you want to go.

Lead your way and create the career you want.

ACKNOWLEDGMENTS

This book has been a labor of love. It has been hard work to put my thoughts down on paper, and I have persevered because of my belief that everyone deserves the chance to have a fulfilling career. The world is not fair—there are people who by birth or instinct know what they need to do to move ahead, and there are many others who do not have access to this information. This book is my attempt to help level the playing field for everyone.

There have been many people who have inspired, encouraged, and supported me in my career and throughout the writing of this book. I owe them a debt of gratitude for helping me bring this book to fruition.

I want to first thank David A. Thomas for his pioneering work in this field, for sharing his wisdom and friendship with me over the years, and for his uncanny ability to expand my world and my thinking.

I want to thank Freada Kapor Klein, who introduced me to the field of diversity and inclusion over 25 years ago. Her work as an activist, researcher, author, investor, and philanthropist is unparalleled.

Another pioneer in the field who I deeply appreciate is J.D. Hokoyama, who recognized the need for more Asian leaders in this country and led the charge to inspire and develop leaders in the Asian community.

I have been blessed to work with incredible people at my client companies—I cannot list all of them, and want to acknowledge just a few of them here. A heartfelt thank you to the following people: Linda Hassan, Manisha Mehrotra, Joan McKinnon, Kimm Maugeri, Michael Molinaro, Ginny Martello, Lance LaVergne, Joanne Rodgers, Kathleen Navarro, Richard Berlin,

Amy Shang, Vance Young, Erica Bolden, Channda Douglas, Maria Merchan, Rachel Skaistis, Kiisha Morrow, Stuart Gold, Lauren Campbell, Lina Maglara, Bobbi Jo Brusco, Dina Salvatore, Kristen Chambers, Linda Akutagawa, Grace Toy, Nancy Yap, Megan Hauck, and Maggie Maxwell. A special thank you to Lisa Ong, who has been a constant source of support and encouragement from the very beginning of this book project.

I have loved working on the Career Management Initiative over the years and have been honored to work with the incredible participants in this program. To each and every one of you—I appreciate and acknowledge you. You have been my inspiration for this book. Every time we started a new cohort, my resolve to finish this book was renewed.

Thank you to my friends and colleagues who have encouraged and supported me on this journey. Thank you to: Tanya Lewis, Nan Mutnick, Susan Collins, Irene Kacandes, Marcia Hamelin, Jenny Levin, Blair Relf, Neena Newberry, Jeanne Jang, Jane Kobayashi, Helen Hayase, Audrey Cahn, Phebe Arlen, and Rosemarie Franzo.

It truly takes a village to publish a book. I'd like to thank my publishing team—my book coach Donna Kozik, project managers Bethany Kelly and Regina Banker, editor Jessica Epstein, and cover designer Stefan Merour.

My family has been a source of love, encouragement, support, and inspiration throughout my life. My Dad and Mom, George and Madge Watai, made everything possible for me. They were both the first in their families to go to college. They forged their own careers and lives without the benefit of a book like this one. They had their challenges, and they never let them drag us down. My brother Jay was my playmate and protector when I was little, and continues to be my best friend and supporter to this day.

I want to thank and acknowledge my children—Scott, Alex, and Elizabeth Lefever. They have supported me in the writing of this book by reading drafts and giving me feedback, and by their constant encouragement and willingness to help me in any way possible. My world is infinitely brighter and more joyful because of them. They inspire me and I learn from them every day.

ABOUT THE AUTHOR

Karen J. Watai is the Founder and President of Welcome Change LLC, a firm that partners with organizations and individuals to achieve results in the areas of leadership, career development, diversity, and inclusion.

Karen is a Master Certified Coach with more than 30 years of business experience. Prior to founding Welcome Change LLC, Karen spent almost 20 years in investment banking and private equity. She was a Vice President at Goldman Sachs and a Partner in the Exeter Group of Funds.

Karen holds an M.B.A. from the University of Chicago Booth School of Business, a J.D. from the University of Chicago Law School, and an A.B. from Harvard University.

Karen lives just outside of New York City, and is often in the city working with clients and seeing Broadway shows.

For more information or to contact Welcome Change LLC, please email info@welcomechange.com

Made in the USA
Monee, IL
03 April 2021

63548109R00095